LET'S TALK
MATH

LET'S TALK
MATH

Encouraging
Children to
Explore Ideas

Pat Lilburn ◆ Pam Rawson

HEINEMANN
Portsmouth, NH

For Michael, David, Timothy and Daniel

HEINEMANN
A division of Reed Elsevier Inc.
361 Hanover Street Portsmouth, NH 03801-3912
Offices and agents throughout the world

First published 1993 by
Oxford University Press
253 Normanby Road
South Melbourne
Victoria, Australia 3205

Library of Congress Cataloging-in-Publication Data
Lilburn, Pat.
    [Talking maths]
    Let's talk math: encouraging children to explore ideas / Pat Lilburn, Pam Rawson.
        p. cm.
    Includes bibliographical references.
    ISBN 0-435-08348-1
    1. Mathematics—Study and teaching (Elementary) I. Rawson, Pam.
II. Title.
QA135.5.L52 1994
372.7'044—dc20   93-44870
                                                            CIP

Cover design by Jenny Jensen Greenleaf
Printed in the United States of America on acid free paper
99 98 97 96 95 94 CC 1 2 3 4 5 6 7 8 9

Contents

ACKNOWLEDGEMENTS

Our thanks go to Tina Diamandis (a teacher who doesn't need to be convinced about the benefits of children talking in maths classes) for her valuable comments about the activities that appear in this book.

We also thank Wendy Maan for her enthusiasm and assistance.

We are grateful to the students and teachers at Orchard Grove Primary School, Eltham College and Kingsville Primary School who trialled activities and responded with such enthusiasm.

Finally, we want to thank Mike and Vasel without whose continued support there would be no book.

Pat Lilburn and Pam Rawson

ABOUT THIS BOOK

How often have you asked a question during your math class, listened to a child's incorrect response and not known what to say to help? So often, in this situation, we simply move on to other children until we get the answer we want to hear. There is nothing wrong with doing this if our main aim is simply to get to the end of the lesson. But if we really want to help children, we must learn how to turn these incorrect responses into opportunities for children to discover more about mathematics. We must let the children tell us how they worked out their answer and we must use this information to assist them to develop an accurate strategy. As teachers we also need to think about the way we ask children questions—do we only want the 'right' answer or do we value *how* the children find their answers? By spending more time finding out how they get their answer, we will encourage children to talk about their mathematical ideas and reasoning.

The *National Statement on Mathematics for Australian Schools* states that

'Students should learn to use language as a tool for reflecting on their mathematical experiences and hence for their own mathematical learning. Explaining to oneself, 'putting it into words', can be a powerful means of working through and clarifying ideas. Mathematical concepts are not developed in the absence of mathematical language. Students are likely to develop mathematical ideas more readily when they have clear ways of labeling and talking about their experiences . . . Students can be encouraged to practise their own use of the language by describing experiences orally and in writing.' (p. 19).

Let's Talk Math will help achieve this goal. The activities in this book are designed so that children will talk and write mathematically. The children are encouraged to talk about and share their ideas, to use everyday language to describe mathematical situations and to restate problems in their own words. Without exception, the teachers we asked to trial these activities commented that it was amazing how much talking about math the activities generated.

There are two sections in this book. Part I talks about some of the issues we feel are important and discusses the implications of these for classroom organisation and planning. Part II introduces 40 activities and describes successful teaching approaches for each one. These activities are related to all areas of the mathematics curriculum. You can choose any one of these activities as your starting point or you can work through them in order as a regular part of your classroom program.

We have used these activities with children from grades 3 to 6. We have also adapted some of them to use with grade 2 children. Before doing any activity with your grade, read it through carefully and adapt it if necessary. For example, most grade 3 and 4 children will not be ready to deal with the larger numbers in 'Millionaire' and 'Writing numbers'. This does not mean you should ignore these activities—simply adapt them by using smaller numbers.

I | Let the talk begin

TODAY'S CLASSROOM

Mathematics thinking has undergone a period of change over the last few years. As with language teaching, teachers' interest in maths has increased. They have been searching for ways to motivate students to enjoy maths and develop confidence in its use. We have seen the emergence of approaches such as

- problem solving
- language and mathematics
- real-life maths
- modelling and technology
- estimation
- mental strategies
- whole maths.

All these approaches have highlighted important and valuable aspects of good mathematics teaching. We believe that all these approaches are important and that each has a fundamental part to play in a teaching program.

However, each of these approaches depends on oral and written language. For example, for children to communicate the range of mental strategies they use, they must rely on language. Discussing work strategies with a partner is a major element of problem solving. As such, language can be the key to learning and teaching. It gives us valuable information about where the children are at, as well as insights into their understanding. Our aim in this book is to show teachers how to make the best use of children's oral language in classroom activities. Having worked through the activities in this book, teachers will have the confidence to apply the same approach in other classroom maths activities.

A MEANINGFUL CONTEXT FOR LEARNING

If we want children to be involved and talk about what they are doing, we must provide a meaningful context for learning. You only have to listen to a group of children in the playground talking about what they did during the weekend to realise the power of a meaningful context for sharing ideas. If we want children to show the same enthusiasm in a classroom we must provide activities that are interesting, challenging and relevant. That is, we need to

- base maths on real situations
- choose activities relevant to the children's experiences
- use activities related to the children's interests

- use a variety of materials and resources
- encourage children to tackle problems in their own way
- be flexible in the way we group children for different activities
- learn to listen to what children have to say
- encourage risk-taking and learning from errors
- value children's thinking.

If we can include all these elements in our maths program we are well on the way to ensuring effective learning.

UNDERSTANDING

As mentioned earlier, teachers can only find out whether children can use mental strategies accurately by letting them *tell* what was going on in their mind as they worked out their solution to a problem. Furthermore, through the discussion of activities teachers will find out whether children really understand mathematical concepts. Understanding concepts involves more than learning a set of rules or using a formula. It involves knowing what method to choose, how to use it and why it works in each situation. It means being able to *use* maths, rather than just reciting it. Some children can perform complicated examples of the addition algorithm, but when confronted with an actual situation that requires addition, they have no idea which of the four processes to use to find an answer. For these children their addition skills are of little value. What is done in the classroom must be real maths, not just school maths. This is not to say that rote learning and blackboard practice examples have no place in a maths program. It is simply to say that when they are used, it should be to consolidate the children's understanding of a developed mathematical concept.

In a grade 4 classroom we planned to ask the children to find a number less than 50 that they would reach when they counted by sixes and also when they counted by eights. When discussing this before the lesson with the classroom teacher, he looked very doubtful and told us quite definitely that the children had not yet been taught to count by sixes or eights and therefore would not be able to do this problem. We said we would like to try it anyway. Working in groups, the children came up with various ways of finding a solution. Some groups found two solutions. Some groups coloured in squares on a hundreds chart, others wrote down the numbers to 50 and marked off every sixth, then every eighth number. Some used their 3 and 4 times tables knowledge. All groups experienced success at this activity. As their teacher commented: 'It didn't matter that they had not been taught to count by sixes or eights, did it? I'm sure they will remember this activity and most of them seem to be well on the way to remembering the counting sequences now.'

By beginning with a problem or a challenge, the children had made a good start to building up a picture of the six and eight number sequences. If we had spent this time on rote counting activities the children would not have developed any strategies which are so necessary for an understanding of counting.

For these children, it would be quite reasonable to spend some time during the next few maths sessions developing automatic recall of these counting sequences through games, drills and so on.

LANGUAGE: THE IMPORTANCE OF TALKING AND RECORDING MATHS

'It may be that in our haste to move students along to the most refined level of mathematical symbolism we leave out the critical step of providing opportunity for conversation, discussion, challenging one's own guesses and having them tested by other members of the group . . . interactive talk. A lot of cognitive reorganisation goes on during these opportunities for talk.' (The *Mathematics Framework P-10*, p. 23).

Children talking together in groups to refine ideas or reach decisions have become a natural part of language, social education, science and other curriculum areas. But in many schools the maths lessons are conducted in near silence. It is as if a different approach to teaching and learning swings into operation. It has no relation to the lessons that come before or after it.

Children do not benefit when teachers shift into a different teaching mode when the maths lesson starts. As in other curriculum areas children need to clarify ideas by talking about them. Think about a situation you have been in where you were unsure about something or needed to decide between several options. What most of us do is sound out the people whose opinions we value and test these against our own. We probably toss the idea around in our own minds, looking at it from these different viewpoints until we reach our final choice. Once we have been through this process we are usually satisfied that we have reached a reasoned decision.

We should provide children with the opportunity to go through a similar process to clarify their mathematical thinking. This means that our classrooms during maths lessons will have children working and talking together in the same way they do in other lessons.

If we are to present maths as an aspect of the real world, we must do this by using the language we use to describe the real world. This means presenting maths so that it is related to children's experiences. They must be allowed to talk about the concepts involved and clarify their ideas in their own language before they can be expected to record their thinking in symbols. For example, when children in a grade 1 class are presented with the example $2 + [\ ] = 6$, many of them will write the answer 8. But if you hide 4 counters under one hand and hold 2 counters in the palm of your other hand so the children can see them, and you say, 'I have really got 6 counters altogether. How many have I got hidden in this hand?', most of the children will be able to work out that the missing addend is 4. Only after children have had many opportunities to talk about and work out situations like this, should we expect them to write down, or read, examples in symbolic form.

It is often the case that children do not understand what they are reading. Their poor comprehension skills can be a barrier to understanding. Many children are handed worksheets that contain ideas well within their grasp, but they are unable to answer any of the questions because they cannot interpret what is being asked. This is not a lack of mathematical knowledge, but a problem of language ability. Unfortunately it is often interpreted as a lack of maths ability. Because children interpret written words in different ways it is important to make sure that all children know what they are doing before they start. We can do this by having questions or statements read out aloud by different children and then, after discussion and sharing ideas, have children restate the problem or task in their own words—thus using everyday language to describe mathematical situations.

HOW TO GET STARTED IN YOUR CLASSROOM

Planning

When you first try something different in your classroom it helps to be able to discuss it with another teacher. Not only will you be able to share some of the preparation, but it is a great support to have someone with whom you can share your successful days and your not so successful days. When we talk about our bad days with another teacher they never seem as bad! When you have this type of support it is far easier to keep trying something that you otherwise may have been tempted to abandon.

Time

All these activities can be fitted into your normal maths program. We suggest you try one activity every two weeks in a regular maths session. After trying a few you will realise that they are not 'extras'—they support your normal program.

Choose an activity that relates to your current area of study. The chart on page 14 will help you make a suitable selection. For example, if you are doing Space, you might choose from activities 13, 24, 26 or 27. If you are doing Fractions, choose from activities 3, 15 or 37. If you are studying a theme, hunt through the activities and you will most likely find something that relates to your theme.

When you first start these activities you will probably find that you follow the lesson plans very closely. As you gain confidence you will find yourself changing the plans to suit your and the children's interests and needs. You may even find that you need to allow more time on another day for children to follow up some aspect that they are particularly interested in.

In many activities you will see that some time is allowed for sharing ideas with the rest of the class. You will notice that this is not always at the end of an activity—sometimes it is during the activity. This is because sharing ideas can often be more effective early in a lesson, especially when groups are trying to work out strategies. There is no point in having a share time if its only purpose is to fill in time at the end of a lesson, as has happened in many process writing sessions.

Classroom environment

You will need to arrange your classroom so that it is conducive to talk. You need a large open area where children can sit comfortably for class discussions. The desks or tables should be positioned so that children can work in groups easily. Any arrangement needs to be flexible—a mix of tables and desks is a good idea.

Make sure you set aside space to display maths work done by the children, for example the findings of group investigations, summaries of class discussions, models made by children etc. Too often in classrooms maths is the only subject not on display. Having maths on display shows children that you value the maths work they have done.

Organise your storage areas so that the children have easy access to the materials they need. Make sure you keep adequate supplies of much used items and check the repairs of others. This will allow you to spend more time on mathematical issues instead of organisational tasks. It also helps the children develop independence.

The teacher's role

Try to remember that your major role during these activities is to encourage children to talk about and share their ideas, to use everyday language to describe mathematical situations and to restate problems in their own words. Try to avoid only saying 'No' or 'Yes' in response to a child's answer. Instead, try asking how or why they reached that answer. Don't influence what they say. Body language, such as a nod of the head or raising our eyebrows can give away what we are thinking in many instances. Remember that it is important for you to find out what the children are thinking and not what they think you want to hear, so that you can use this information to diagnose problem areas and so assist the children. If you can manage to do this, you will have gone a long way towards letting children know that you value all their ideas, not just a correct answer.

You must also make the children aware of what you are trying to do so that they have a clear expectation of their role. Each of the activities in Part II should be presented in the way it is outlined. Although you will probably write each problem on the chalkboard or a chart so the children can read them easily, this does not mean they should be presented as chalkboard exercises or they will become simply 'busy work' and their value will be lost. Do not panic if your children seem to spend most of their time talking during these sessions, without 'getting anything down on paper'. *Remember*: children must be allowed to talk about concepts and clarify their ideas in their own language before they can be expected to record their thinking in symbols.

Stop and listen to some groups talking and you will be reassured that the maths learning that is taking place has more value than most chalkboard exercises. When groups are working well, try not to interrupt them. Let them realise that it is their responsibility to take control of what they are doing, not yours. When it is necessary to work with a group, your role is to help that group solve its own problems, not to solve it for them.

Classroom management

Before you start these activities, you may want to let the children know that this is something different that you or they have not tried before. We did this when we first started and found the response really positive. The children were excited to think they were sharing in an adventure with us.

If the children are not used to working in co-operative groups, you will most likely need to have a few sessions which simply establish the rules for group work and allow children time to practise some of the skills required to work effectively as a group. Start off with some simple and basic rules that will get your groups working effectively. You will be able to refine and add to these rules as you go. Following are some of the basic rules that we found useful to begin with:

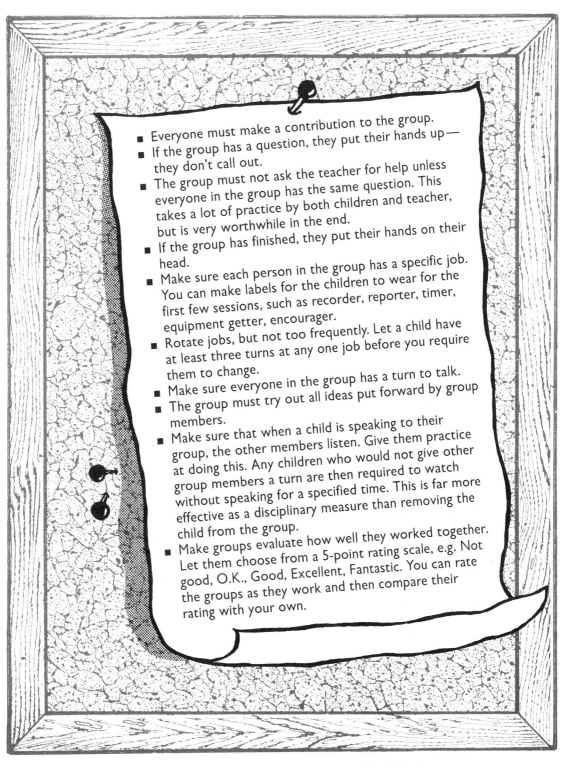

- Everyone must make a contribution to the group.
- If the group has a question, they put their hands up— they don't call out.
- The group must not ask the teacher for help unless everyone in the group has the same question. This takes a lot of practice by both children and teacher, but is very worthwhile in the end.
- If the group has finished, they put their hands on their head.
- Make sure each person in the group has a specific job. You can make labels for the children to wear for the first few sessions, such as recorder, reporter, timer, equipment getter, encourager.
- Rotate jobs, but not too frequently. Let a child have at least three turns at any one job before you require them to change.
- Make sure everyone in the group has a turn to talk.
- The group must try out all ideas put forward by group members.
- Make sure that when a child is speaking to their group, the other members listen. Give them practice at doing this. Any children who would not give other group members a turn are then required to watch without speaking for a specified time. This is far more effective as a disciplinary measure than removing the child from the group.
- Make groups evaluate how well they worked together. Let them choose from a 5-point rating scale, e.g. Not good, O.K., Good, Excellent, Fantastic. You can rate the groups as they work and then compare their rating with your own.

Be prepared for more noise than you would normally accept! Initially, children will be excited and when they are talking in groups the noise level may increase. However, if children are too noisy for your liking make it clear from the outset what level you will tolerate and remind them frequently.

When you first start the activities allow yourself and the children time to adjust to the different style of working. Realise that many children have never experienced this style before and may feel insecure. It often takes a few lessons and a few successes to feel confident.

One question that we are frequently asked, is 'What do I do with children who finish early?'. This can occur in any lesson and well-prepared teachers generally have other things ready for children to go on with. However, it is worth mentioning that it is generally not necessary or even desirable for all the groups to finish the activity before the teacher concludes the lesson with a sharing time. If we are focusing on strategies rather than an answer, then all the groups will be able to contribute to the share time by telling what their group had talked about.

Sometimes groups will not have got very far even though they have worked hard. There is nothing wrong with this—sometimes we walk out of meetings without any decisions having been made either! If the groups want to continue working, then organise another time that suits both you and them. Sometimes groups will not want to finish a task. This is also all right as long as you are satisfied that they have worked well. There are no hard and fast rules for situations such as these. You will have to decide how to treat them as they arise.

For those who do finish early, try these suggestions:

- Ask the children to rate how they worked as a group.
- Ask the children to prepare for share time. This way they reflect on what they have done and are better prepared to contribute.
- Ask the children to make a chart or poster about how they solved the problem.
- Ask the group to make up a similar problem.
- Have a 'problem for the week' on display for them to go on with.
- Have a 'lucky dip' box of problems.
- Have a problem corner with a selection of tasks for them to choose from.

Grouping

If you want children to get the most out of discussion activities, they must be working in effective co-operative groups. If this style of learning is new to your children you will need to spend some time to teach them how to work this way. As Joan Dalton says, 'It takes time, guidance, and encouragement to teach children to work in small groups, and for the vast majority of children this involves learning skills.'. (Joan Dalton, *Adventures in Thinking*, Thomas Nelson Australia, 1991, p. 12)

As previously stated, many of the activities in this book are most suitable for co-operative group work. Many are open-ended, thus ensuring that all children are challenged and successful in some way. In some activities you will find it best for the children to work in pairs. At other times you may want the children working in larger groups. Make sure your groups are small enough so that everyone has a chance to contribute. We suggest that you never have more than six children in a group.

There are various ways of grouping children:

- friendship groups
- interest groups
- skills groups

- similar-ability groups
- mixed-ability groups.

The most effective grouping for these maths activities is the mixed-ability grouping. The different attitudes and opinions that each child contributes give this group its effectiveness.

It is also important for us to recognise the differences between traditional classroom groupings and co-operative groups so that we give children the chance to take responsibility for their own learning, to interact with others and to understand that everyone contributes in some way.

Co-operative groups don't just happen. Before you expect children to work in co-operative groups, you need to teach them the necessary skills, such as:

- collecting and packing up equipment
- listening to and valuing others' ideas
- helping others in the group
- being responsible for their own behaviour
- encouraging others in the group
- taking turns.

How long this takes will depend on whether the children have worked in this way before. It is obvious that much effort will be required before the children can effectively share tasks, work towards the group goal, develop self-evaluation skills and share in the group's successes and failures.

When you are satisfied that the groups are ready to start work on the activities, you need to consider how long each group should be allowed to work together. We suggest at least for four activities. This allows children within each group to develop a group identity and recognise and use the skills of group members.

Most importantly, do not expect perfection the first time, if at all. If you are ready to despair, think about some of the adult groups you work with and how difficult it can be at times. Too often we have heard teachers say about a game, excursion or activity, 'I am not doing that again. The children were terrible and could not do it properly.'. If those teachers would only think about what they said, they would realise that it was in fact a very good reason for repeating the activity. We cannot expect children to become proficient unless they are given practice.

EVALUATION

Evaluation is an important part of the overall success of a teaching program. We need to keep evaluation records so that

- we can check that children are learning: Teachers usually have a very accurate idea of what mathematical skills a child has, e.g. whether the child can perform the procedure of subtraction involving zeros. However, teachers are less likely to have the same accurate picture about whether the child understands enough about subtraction to apply the process in a real situation. Therefore our records need to be more than just skills checklists to give a true picture of each child's progress.
- we can provide children with appropriate feedback: If we want children to take responsibility and to value the work they do in maths, it is only fair that

we provide them with feedback. This feedback should always be positive and encouraging, but there is no value to either the child or the teacher if it is not accurate and honest—which means that if a child's work is not up to scratch, they need to know. Provide feedback as frequently as needed—not just at the end of a session or a term. It is more effective if it is provided early on rather than after the work has been done. It can then be used to help children plan further work.

- we can report children's progress to their parents or other teachers.
- we can see any areas of concern regarding course content and coverage: We need to know that we are providing a balanced program that covers all aspects of the maths curriculum. If we don't keep a record of the objectives for the year, we may neglect some parts of the curriculum.

How do we evaluate?

There are various ways of collecting and recording information for evaluation purposes. Here are some ideas that have worked for us.

1 Course content

At the beginning of the year, list the content areas you will be covering throughout the year. You can find these in curriculum documents and your school policy. Keep this in your record-keeping book (or appropriate part of your work program). For each maths activity you plan for your class, including the ones you use from this book, enter it in the left-hand column of the grid and then tick off the content areas covered by the activity. If you do this consistently you will build up an accurate picture of the content areas you have covered and how much emphasis you are placing on each area. Areas you are neglecting will be obvious and you should choose activities to redress this. The chart on page 14 tells you the content areas covered by each of the activities in this book.

2 Anecdotal records

We found it useful to prepare a set of class lists which we kept on a clipboard within easy reach. We would use one list per fortnight and then start a new sheet. We used these sheets to record behaviours that were important to the style of learning operating in our classroom and not just as skills checklists. As soon as we observed a child showing that they understood a concept, or finally taking turns at sharing, or planning their own investigation for the first time, we wrote it down on the sheet beside their name. This set of sheets built up a rounded profile of the children and was put to good use when writing reports and at parent/teacher interviews.

Names	Comments
Sophia	12/6 Reported her group's findings for the first time
Nicholas	14/6 Described a 3's pattern on a hundreds chart.
Carla	15/6 Used mathematical terms confidently to describe the shape.

It will be useful to have a class list like this at hand while working through any of the activities from this book. The language used by the children while they are doing these activities will provide a rich source of anecdotal comments.

3 Class checklists

We found class checklists to be a useful summary of skills mastered by the children. Ours were based on three categories: mathematical skills, group working skills and social skills. When a child demonstrated a skill, the appropriate box beside their name was ticked. When three ticks appeared in a box it was coloured in to show that the child had mastered the skill and applied it consistently.

We found it very important to limit ourselves to these three forms of evaluation. They are accurate and comprehensive without being a burden to maintain. There is no point in setting up so many records that you have to use up valuable class time collecting the information to fill them out, rather than working with the children.

You will notice that we have not mentioned the traditional class written maths test. These tests are fine for checking on a child's ability to reproduce mathematical procedures. But the best place to see if a child can do something is to observe them while they are doing it. For example, you would not choose a dentist on the basis of a written test on extracting teeth; you would rather know that they had actually done it, successfully!

Exploring ideas

INTRODUCTION TO THE ACTIVITIES

Each of the activities in this section starts by introducing the problem, and then develops further under three headings:

Curriculum links

This tells you what maths concepts are dealt with in the activity and provides a basic background to the task.

Discussing and solving the problem

This outlines how the lesson may develop and provides some of the student responses we have had in our classrooms. We do not present each activity as a step-by-step lesson plan. To do so would limit your responses to the children's creativity. You may, however, find the guidelines opposite useful for assistance with your lesson planning.

Building on the activity

This talks about ways you can extend or adapt the activity for your students and their needs.

---

9 Hot chips

The cook at a school camp is working out his food order for the next month. He likes to make chips and knows that they are a favourite with most children. He calculates that he will need 49 kilograms of potatoes to feed everyone. When he goes to the store to buy the potatoes he finds that they are already packed and come in either 3-kg or 5-kg bags. He does not want to buy any more than 49 kilograms. How can he get the exact amount that he needs?

Curriculum links

This would be a good activity to do just before children go on a school camp. The activity could lead on to other investigations, for example: How many chips can be made from one potato? How many potatoes are there in 49 kilograms? How much would this many potatoes cost? How long does it take to cook chips? People's favourite ways to eat potatoes etc. This shows the possibilities for links with mass, money, time and graphing. We are sure you can think of many more.

DISCUSSING AND SOLVING THE PROBLEM

Most children find it hard to visualise 49 kilograms of potatoes. We showed our groups a one-kilogram bag and counted the number of potatoes in it so that they would gain a better understanding of the amount involved. This generated much discussion about how many potatoes there would be in 49 kilograms and provided an excellent opportunity for some estimation.

Once you are satisfied that the children understand the question, set them to work in groups to find some answers. Many groups we worked with tried initially to see if they could buy the potatoes all in 3-kg bags or all in 5-kg bags. When they found that they couldn't, they used trial and error to work it out and were satisfied when they found one answer. To reach a total of 49 kilograms, one group we watched approached the problem in a systematic way by making a table like the one opposite.

By the time they had finished they found three possible solutions and knew that they had found them all.

The groups who worked on a trial-and-error basis had difficulty in finding more than one solution.

32

We have 5-kg bags	We still need	3-kg bags
1 (= 5 kg)	44 kg	can't do
2 (= 10 kg)	39 kg	13 (= 49 kg)
3 (= 15 kg)	34 kg	can't do
4 (= 20 kg)	29 kg	can't do
5 (= 25 kg)	24 kg	8 (= 49 kg)
6 (= 30 kg)	19 kg	can't do
7 (= 35 kg)	14 kg	can't do
8 (= 40 kg)	9 kg	3 (= 49 kg)
9 (= 45 kg)	4 kg	can't do

BUILDING ON THE ACTIVITY

❑ When the children have finished, let each group tell the others how they worked out their answer. If no groups have done it systematically, do it together on the chalkboard. You can start with the 5-kg bags or the 3-kg bags.

❑ Present the groups with a similar problem and ask them to work it out by making a table like the one you have on the chalkboard. A similar problem could be 67 kilograms of potatoes available in either 7-kg or 3-kg bags.

Once children saw the chart they could hardly wait to get started on a similar activity.

33

Planning guidelines

You should always begin each activity by following the four steps in Stage 1 (see below). This is important so that all the children are quite clear about what it is that they are going to do. It also gives you a good opportunity to find out their current level of understanding of the concepts involved when they try to explain in their own words what the question is asking them to do. Each of the steps within Stages 2, 3 and 4 are in a suggested sequence. You may find that you need to change their order, depending on the activity you are doing. We find it is important not to always leave the share time until the end, but to deliberately make times during the lesson for groups or children to share what they are doing at the moment. This is often a way to spark up other groups that have run into a dead end.

STAGE 1 **Defining the task**
a   Children read the problem silently.
b   Ask two or three children to read the problem out loud.
c   Ask a child or two to explain the problem in their own words.
d   Reach class agreement about what the task is.

STAGE 2 **Strategies**
a   In groups, the children talk about the task and work out how they will find their answer.
b   Discuss these strategies as a class.
c   Let each group decide if they want to revise their approach.

STAGE 3 **Towards a solution**
Children work in groups to find their answer(s), using their chosen approach.

STAGE 4 **Sharing the task**
Give each group time to tell the class what they have done and what else they could do now.

Maths content	Rabbits	What's missing?	Chocolate biscuits	Dice toss	Floor tiles	The icing on the cake	Ben's new clothes	Holidays	Hot chips	Building fences	Football jumpers	Spending money	Shop display	Parking fees	Flags	Business sense	Make one metre	Theatre tickets	Duty rosters
Counting	●	●			●	●										●			
Place value											●								
Operations	●	●		●				●				●	●			●	●	●	
Fractions & decimals			●												●				
Pattern & order	●	●		●	●	●	●						●		●	●	●	●	●
Length										●							●		
Perimeter										●									
Area				●											●				
Volume						●													
Mass									●										
Money				●					●			●		●				●	
Time									●					●					●
Visual representation									●										●
Chance																			
Space		●		●	●					●			●						

14

Activities

Maths content	Wheeling & dealing	Popular letters	Millionaire	Writing numbers	Running race	Letter writing	Sheep pens	Making posters	Lunch-time	Good news travels fast	Bells	Rescue attempt	Water jugs	Wages	Postage	Mystery story	Parking lot	Pocket money	Roll out the red carpet	Knock-out	Round robins
Counting		●		●		●				●											
Place value				●																	
Operations	●		●	●		●			●		●				●	●	●		●		●
Fractions & decimals																		●			
Pattern & order						●	●			●	●			●						●	●
Length								●													
Perimeter					●			●											●		
Area																	●		●		
Volume													●								
Mass																					
Money	●		●						●					●	●			●			
Time			●		●					●											
Visual representation		●										●									
Chance		●																			
Space							●	●									●				

1 **Rabbits**

Mother Rabbit woke one morning and looked around her to see if all her baby rabbits were safe. She tried to count them, but the burrow was so cramped and the rabbits were snuggled together so tightly that the best she could do was count all the legs and ears she could see. She counted ten more legs than ears and so she knew that all her bunnies were safe. How many baby rabbits did she have?

Curriculum links

Most children have a very clear picture of the situation but are convinced that they have not been given enough information to answer the question. Once they have been helped to devise a strategy for finding an answer, they begin to see a range of interrelated number patterns emerging. This activity will provide good practice with counting and number relationships. Most children find that the solution to the initial activity is in fact quite simple and are keen to play around with other possible number patterns in this scenario to create related problems of their own.

DISCUSSING AND SOLVING THE PROBLEM

Even after they have read through the problem silently two or three times, most children cannot understand how the mother rabbit can know that all her babies are safe. You will have no trouble in finding children who can explain what it is they have to work out. But if you ask them for a way of working out an answer, the best they seem to offer at this stage is random guessing.

Put them in groups and tell them to think of a way to work out the answer. Once the children work out an effective strategy, the solution to the original question quickly becomes apparent. (Ask them to keep their answer secret to give the other groups more incentive to keep working.) This process does not usually take them too long, so every group should have time to find a strategy and an answer. At share time you will probably find that there are a number of ways for children to reach the correct answer of 5 rabbits.

Following are some possible responses:

■ Some children will have used pencil and paper to draw up a table similar to the one opposite. This provides an excellent format for discussing the number patterns involved.

Rabbits	Legs	Ears	How many more legs than ears?
1	4	2	2
2	8	4	4
3	12	6	6
4	16	8	8
5	20	10	10

- Some groups we worked with drew a line of rabbits and used these to work out how many were needed to have 10 more legs than ears.
- Some children started hopping around being bunnies while one member of their group counted legs and ears.
- Some groups do in fact find their answer by random guesswork. (It is important for these groups to see that there are more efficient strategies that provide more information, otherwise these children will have great difficulty in tackling any of the related activities that follow.)
- Sometimes a group will summarise the problem by saying that each rabbit has 2 more legs than ears, so that if there are 10 more legs than ears there must be 5 rabbits.

BUILDING ON THE ACTIVITY

❑ If the table of information illustrated above does not come to light during share time, have the children help you compile a similar one on the chalkboard. Ask questions about the number relationships involved. For example: If there are 16 legs, how many ears should there be? (8). Is it possible to have 20 more legs than ears? (Yes). Why? What other numbers are possible? (Any even number). What numbers are not possible? (Odd numbers).

❑ Ask the children to solve a related problem. Tell them that the following morning the mother rabbit could only see legs and cottontails. She counted 12 more legs than cottontails. Were all her rabbits there? (No, one of the 5 was missing.)
Put the children in groups to work this one out and allow plenty of time for them to explain their strategies and solutions and the difference in the number patterns involved in this question and the previous one. (There are 3 more legs than cottontails for each rabbit.)

❑ In pairs, ask the children to make up a similar problem about any kind of animal (e.g. using legs and wings on bees, legs and eyes on octopuses, trunks and legs on an elephant etc.). They should write their problem on a sheet of paper and illustrate it so it can become part of a class book.

The power of group work is confirmed when a seemingly impossible problem is quickly solved when everyone contributes their ideas.

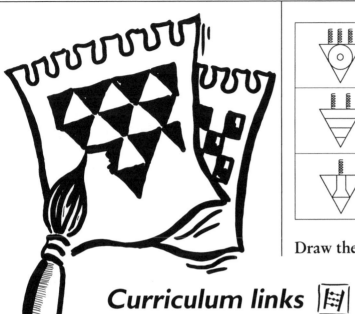

⟦2⟧ What's missing?

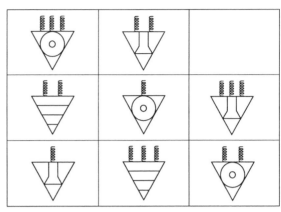

Draw the missing shape.

Curriculum links 🏁 ▦ 🖩 🫛

Some children are initially baffled by this task, but by talking together in groups they soon begin to pick up the separate elements in each figure—the squiggles and the shape—and begin to see patterns. All children manage to find enough patterns to help them find the missing shape. Most are very surprised though when they hear of all the other patterns that other children have found. Rarely does one child see all the patterns contained in the grid and the children sense that it has been a joint class effort to find all the possible patterns.

DISCUSSING AND SOLVING THE PROBLEM

Give each pair of children a copy of page 96 and let them look at the shapes on the grid. Ask them what patterns they can see. You will receive plenty of answers, but do not go into too much detail at this stage—just enough to make sure that all children can see the possibilities.

Now tell the children to work out what the missing shape looks like and to draw it in. Some pairs will be ready to do this immediately, others will need a little more time. When most pairs have finished, let them show their solution to the rest of the class and say why they have drawn the shape they did. Accept all shapes that the children can justify. You will find during this share time that some pairs will change their minds—allow them to alter their shape if they wish.

BUILDING ON THE ACTIVITY

❏ Give each pair a copy of the blank grid on page 97 and tell them to place this edge to edge with their completed pattern so that the lines match. (It doesn't matter if they join it at the side or at the bottom.) Tell them to extend their pattern on to the blank grid. When they have done this, let them join their sheets with another pair to make a 4-grid pattern mat. (You can continue this by joining up every pair's sheets to make a giant class pattern.)

❏ You can use the grids to practise number facts. Once the children can see a few of the grids together, ask them to look at the squiggles and count how many are in each row. Ask, 'Does each row have the same number of squiggles? Can you explain why?' Do the same for the columns.

These make a fantastic display on your board, especially if you get the children to colour them in (to make a pattern, of course!).

3   Chocolate biscuits

Everyone in our family loves my mum's chocolate biscuits. Last night while we were watching TV, Mum put out a plate of her biscuits. By bed-time there were none left. Dad had eaten half of them and my older brother had eaten a quarter. Mum had eaten only one and I'd eaten three. We were arguing over how many biscuits Mum had put on the plate to start with. Can you work it out?

Curriculum links

Most children find this fraction problem challenging because they cannot 'connect' the different pieces of information provided. When they try to model the situation with counters or by drawing, they do not know how to represent the half eaten by 'Dad' and the quarter eaten by the 'older brother'. Once they realise that the four biscuits 'Mum and I' ate are the fraction *not* eaten by 'Dad and my older brother', they are able to work out their answer quite quickly.

DISCUSSING AND SOLVING THE PROBLEM

After reading the question through, the children will readily explain that they have to find out how many biscuits were on the plate at the start of the evening. However, many may still be puzzled because they are unable to work out what information they have been given to work from. We put the children in groups and asked them to discuss what information the question provided and to try to show this by using blocks, counters or other available material, or by drawing. After some minutes of discussion there was still a lot of uncertainty among the groups. Most had represented the one biscuit eaten by 'Mum' and the three eaten by 'me' easily enough using pictures or concrete materials, but could not work out how to represent the half and the quarter eaten by 'Dad' and the 'older brother'.

At this point it was suggested that each group start by drawing an empty plate. Having done this, most groups continued to discuss the information with little confidence and much uncertainty for several more minutes, until gradually there came shouts of delight as the different groups realised they could show all the information on the plate.

Most groups drew something like this:

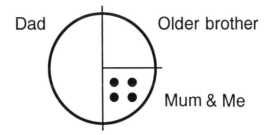

From there it was easy to see that the four biscuits 'Mum' and 'I' ate were $\frac{1}{4}$ of the plateful; that the 'older brother' had also eaten $\frac{1}{4}$ (4 biscuits) and that Dad had eaten twice as many as this (8 biscuits). All these added together gave a total of 16 biscuits.

BUILDING ON THE ACTIVITY

❑ If the children in your class have had some experience with equivalent fractions, you may like to try some variations on this situation, such as:

■ Dad and Mum each ate $\frac{1}{4}$ of the biscuits, my older brother ate $\frac{1}{3}$ and I ate 5.
■ We each ate $\frac{1}{5}$ and there were 3 left.

❑ The children also enjoy making up their own versions of the problem for others in the class to solve.

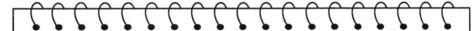

Work backwards! Let the children draw a 'plate diagram' (like the one shown above) to show the solution to their problem. Display three or four solutions with their problem in a random arrangement and let the children work out which solution belongs to which problem.

4 Dice toss

Look at the drawing of the dice. If a dice is tossed to land like this, what is the sum of the numbers you *can't* see?

Curriculum links

This is a marvellous way to practise addition facts to 20. Children are also given opportunities to search for number patterns and to see how the numbers on a dice are arranged. The activity described in the section following is quite easy for some children, however, there are plenty of ways for you to challenge them by using some of the ideas in 'Building on the Activity'.

DISCUSSING AND SOLVING THE PROBLEM

If available, use large dice or else use large MAB blocks and tape on dots to make them resemble dice. This will make it much easier for the children to see.

To start with, have the children sitting so that they all have the same view of the dice (i.e. not in a circle). Roll the dice and make sure that the children can see three dice faces—the top face and two of the side faces. Ask the children what numbers they can see from where they are sitting. Ask them to add these three numbers and tell you the total (this will vary depending on the toss of the dice). Now ask them to work out the total of the three numbers they *cannot* see. It is surprising how many will simply tell you it is the same as the total of the numbers they can see. Younger children will often tell you, 'That's impossible!' They believe that they have to be given more information before they can begin to work out an answer. This is because they have no idea of how a dice is numbered.

Ask the children to form groups and discuss how to work this out. Share the groups' ideas. Turn the dice around and let the children see whether their strategy worked. Then roll the dice again and allow groups to test their strategies on a new set of numbers. Most groups will have figured that they must use the fact that dice are numbered from 1 to 6, work out which numbers cannot be seen and add these up.

BUILDING ON THE ACTIVITY

❑ Now give each group a dice—a small one will do. Ask them to roll a 6. Now ask them to tell you, without lifting the dice, what number is on the bottom. Let children give their answer and explain how they worked it out. Some will just take a lucky guess; many will check what other numbers are visible on the other faces and thus work out which number is missing.

    Let them roll a different number and predict what number is hidden on the opposite face. Give them time to work out a generalisation about the sum of the two numbers on opposite faces of a dice. (They total 7.)

❑ Once children have reached this point, you can have them work out the total of the numbers on a dice and ask them to predict how often the three faces they can see will total more than half this number, i.e. 11 or more. Most will guess about half the time. Have them throw their dice at least 50 times to check their prediction. See if they can explain why this is so.

❑ What is the highest total they can get from the three faces? (15, i.e. 4, 5 and 6.) Now have them predict whether the three numbers not visible in this situation add to the lowest possible total. (They do—the missing numbers will always be 1, 2 and 3.) Give the groups another dice and let them investigate highest and lowest totals for two dice.

> *We were amazed at how many children were completely unfamiliar with the way a dice is numbered.*

5 | Floor tiles

We need tiles for our new bathroom and the hardware store is selling triangular floor tiles on special for $1 each. They have lots of different colours. But there are not enough tiles of any of the colours to cover the whole floor. So we designed a pattern of squares that will use seven different colours. The central square will be made up of four triangular tiles of one colour and each of the larger squares will be a different colour. Now we have to work out how many tiles we have to buy of each colour and how much it is going to cost us altogether. Can you help us?

Curriculum links

It is interesting to watch the range of different strategies children use in trying to work out a solution to this problem. They are usually very surprised to see how other groups reached the same answer as they did using such different methods. This problem can provide the children with valuable practice in number patterns, shape, shape patterns, area and money.

DISCUSSING AND SOLVING THE PROBLEM

Hand each child a copy of page 98 to look at as they read the problem. Give them time to examine the design on the page so they can understand exactly what the question is describing. You may need to ask several children to explain what they are asked to find out so that everyone is quite clear on the task.

Put the children in groups and tell them to discuss among themselves what method they will use to work out an answer, and then to begin work. All the groups we worked with were able to find some means of starting to work towards a solution. (We found it was better not to call the class together to discuss what strategy each group was using, as this resulted in a wide variety of methods being used.)

■ Two groups had fetched coloured paper and were busily folding, cutting and pasting to recreate the pattern so they could count how many triangles of each colour were needed. One of these groups simply cut out one square of each colour, making sure each was the right size to build up the pattern, then ruled the smaller triangles on to this design and started counting. The other group actually cut out piles of triangles for each colour and pasted these into a pattern before they started counting. (This group was the last to finish!)

24

- One group used their copy of page 98 and ruled the small triangles on to each square so they could count these.
- One group set out to look for number patterns using their knowledge of shape and area. They knew that four triangles had been used for the red square. If the four corners of the yellow square are folded into the centre, they cover the red square exactly, so the yellow square also uses 4 triangles. If the four corners of the white square are folded into the centre, they cover the red and white squares exactly, so the white square must use the same number of triangles as the yellow and red squares combined: $4 + 4 = 8$ triangles. The corners of the blue square fold in to cover the three smaller squares, so it must use $8 + 4 + 4 = 16$ triangles.

  At this stage the group was confident they had established the pattern of doubling the number of triangles for each successive square, i.e. the green square needed 32 triangles, the black needed 64 and the orange needed 128. This came to a total of $256 to buy all the tiles needed.

We gave each group extra time to show their method and their solution on a chart or poster suitable for display. When we had our final share time, all the children listened very intently to the methods others had used to solve the problem.

BUILDING ON THE ACTIVITY

❏ Ask the children to use the same number of triangular tiles of each of the colours that were used for the bathroom floor and rearrange these to make a different pattern. The final designs pasted into position on a chart make a wonderful display.

❏ It is worthwhile to try to visit a tiling showroom, or at least collect brochures from different tiling manufacturers, so the children can look at the patterns and even work out the numbers of different tiles needed to make some of the designs shown.

After this activity our children would comment on patterns they noticed, not just in tiles, but in all sorts of building and architectural features.

6 The icing on the cake

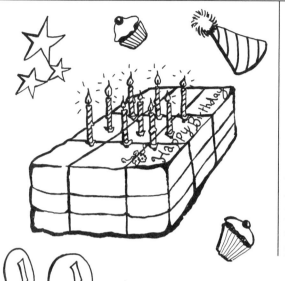

Angie's mother made a delicious sponge cake with chocolate icing for Angie's birthday. There were a lot of people at the party, adults as well as children, so Angie's mother cut the cake into blocks like the cake in the picture so there would be a piece for everyone. Some of the younger children started squabbling about whose piece of cake had the most icing. Can you work out how many pieces of the cake had icing on three sides, how many had icing on two sides, on one side and how many had no icing at all?

Curriculum links

This is a good activity for encouraging the children to make the distinction between area and volume and to look at the different surfaces on a three-dimensional object.

DISCUSSING AND SOLVING THE PROBLEM

Ask several children to explain the information given in the problem. Make sure they realise that the cake is not iced on the bottom surface.

Before setting the children to work on the problem, ask them to count how many pieces of cake there are altogether. Tell them to draw their own diagram if this helps. Ask a number of children to give their answer (27) and their explanation. There will be a great variety in explanations as there are a number of ways to interpret 3-D diagrams. Some children count the blocks in each horizontal layer and multiply this by 3, some count the blocks in each vertical layer, some count the blocks on each end layer, then the outer blocks on the centre 'ring', then the block hidden in the centre.

Once the children have had some practice at interpreting the picture, put them in groups and set them to work. Most children find it difficult to separate their method from their answer in this activity, so it is best not to interrupt them until they have a solution. Encourage the children to work out their answer from the diagram on the chalkboard (or from a copy on their own sheet of paper in front of them). However, if they have real difficulty in doing this, provide them with blocks or modelling clay. When all the groups have an answer, ask one member from each group to report their answer and their explanation to the whole class.

Start a table of results on the chalkboard like this:

3 iced faces	4
2 iced faces	12
1 iced face	9
0 iced faces	2

BUILDING ON THE ACTIVITY

❑ Ask the children to work out what the answers would have been if Angie's mother had cut the cake into a $2 \times 2 \times 2$ block. Then look at the answers for a $4 \times 4 \times 4$ block. Add this information to the table you started on the chalkboard:

	$2 \times 2 \times 2$	$3 \times 3 \times 3$	$4 \times 4 \times 4$
3 iced faces	4	4	4
2 iced faces	4	12	20
1 iced face		9	28
0 iced faces		2	12

❑ Ask the children if they can see any patterns developing. Ask them to predict the answers for a $5 \times 5 \times 5$ block. Draw this and find out the answers. Were the children correct?

Your students will undoubtedly agree that the best way to check these results is to make and ice a chocolate cake, then to cut it into blocks as directed. They rarely have trouble 'packing away' the cake at the end of the activity!

7 | Ben's new clothes

Ben had grown so quickly over the last six months that all his clothes were now too small for him. His mother took him shopping and they bought three new tops, three pairs of pants and two pairs of shoes. By wearing these clothes in different combinations, how many different outfits could Ben make with his new clothes?

Curriculum links

This is a familiar situation that the children readily grasp. They eagerly suggest combinations that will make new outfits, but many of them will need help in working out a strategy that will find all the possibilities. They are usually most impressed when they discover that the solution can be found mathematically and are keen to try this out in related situations.

DISCUSSING AND SOLVING THE PROBLEM

Give each child a copy of page 99. When the children have read through the problem first silently and then out loud, choose several children to explain in their own words what they are being asked to find out. Children are usually eager to explain and give examples of possible new outfits, using the pictures on their sheet.

Put the children in groups. Stress again that their task is to find out all the possible combinations that can be made with the new clothing. Let them start work and move about the room to see what methods they are using. The first problem the groups come up against is how to record the combinations they find.

- Some groups will give each item of clothing a name (e.g. jumper, track pants, jeans, runners, gym boots etc.) and start writing down different combinations of these.
- Some groups will cut out the items of clothing on all the group members' sheets and arrange these on their table in different combinations. (Unless the group is very large they will not have enough pictures to make all the possible solutions.)

- Others will just cut up one sheet and start to make different arrangements with these, recording each combination before shuffling the items and making the next one. (They record each combination by naming each item or by colouring in each of the items a different colour and recording the combinations as three dots of colours.)
- Other groups will simply draw lines linking different combinations of tops/pants/shoes, numbering each line as they go.

Once most of the groups have established their method of recording, stop the whole class for a share time so that groups can decide if theirs is an efficient method and make any changes they feel are necessary. Let them continue working and now watch to see how they arrange their results in order so they can check if they have found all of the (18) possible combinations. Some groups succeed in finding all the combinations in no particular order. The groups who draw lines linking the different combinations usually see the pattern first and are in the best position to explain and justify their answer.

When most groups feel they have exhausted the possibilities, stop for a share time and let each group tell how many combinations they found and ask for volunteers to explain why 18 is the correct answer. At least one of the groups will be able to explain that combining each of the three tops with three different pairs of pants creates $3 \times 3 = 9$ combinations. When each of these is combined first with one pair of shoes, then with the other, the number of combinations is doubled: $3 \times 3 \times 2 = 18$.

BUILDING ON THE ACTIVITY

❏ What would happen if Ben lost one of his new tops? (Now only $2 \times 3 \times 2 = 12$ combinations are possible.) See which children can work this out with numbers only and which children go back to manipulating their pictures.

❏ Would Ben have been better off to buy four tops, only two pairs of pants and two pairs of runners? (No, $4 \times 2 \times 2 = 16$ combinations.)

❏ Let the children try to make up related problems. For example: How many different ice-creams can you make using six different flavours and two types of cones? How many different dolls can you make using two types of hair, three different dresses and either black or white shoes?

Let them present their problem and its solution to the class.

Children will actually apply this information when it's time for them to buy new clothes. You may find yourself involved in family budgeting!

Last holidays we drove from Melbourne to Brisbane to visit our cousins. It was a really long trip and got pretty boring after a while. So Mum gave me the road map and asked me to work out where we should stop to buy petrol. Our car travels only 300 kilometres on a full tank. Can you work out where we should stop to fill the tank?

Curriculum links

Some children become quite worried when working out this problem: they are scared they will run out of petrol in the middle of nowhere! Most children, to begin with, do not realise that it is a very open-ended situation and that the family can stop in every town if they wish to. Once the children realise that they are looking for groups of numbers that are close to 300 (without exceeding it), they quickly work towards a solution. This activity gives the children excellent practice at estimating, adding 2- and 3-digit numbers and using calculators.

DISCUSSING AND SOLVING THE PROBLEM

Give each child a copy of the map on page 100 before they start reading the problem. Give them several minutes to read through the problem and check what information the map provides them with to help work out a solution. Choose several children to explain what they have to find out. Make clear what will happen if they try to exceed 300 kilometres between petrol stops.

Put the children in groups and let them start work. Let them know that calculators are available if they want to use them. All groups quickly work out that their basic strategy must be to add the distances between towns until they get close to 300 kilometres. But agreement usually ends there! Be prepared for heated discussions about whether it is better to stop in one town or another. For example, the children see that they cannot quite get to Albury in one go (Melbourne to Albury = 303 km) but will argue whether to stop in Seymour, then Albury (206 km), or wait until Benalla and try to reach Gundagai from there (267 km). In fact, it doesn't matter which choice is made, but for some reason children will argue very strongly for one case or the other.

If group members cannot resolve their disagreements, it may be best to stop for a whole class discussion to highlight that it doesn't matter how many stops are made, only that they do not exceed 300 km between stops. Emphasise that there are many possible itineraries for the trip. When you send the groups back to work you may find that they can manage to reach agreement—however, quite often some children will choose to plan their own trip independently of the rest of their group.

When they have finished planning their trip, ask one person from each group to describe their journey to the rest of the class and to explain how they decided where to stop. One standard journey woud be: Melbourne—Benalla (193)—Albury (110)—Yass (281)—Sydney (296)—Newcastle (174)—Pt Macquarie (246)—Grafton (252)—Coolangatta (214)—Brisbane (136).

BUILDING ON THE ACTIVITY

❑ Ask the children to plan the return journey. Is it best to stop in the same towns on the way back or is it more convenient to change the trip plan?

> *Be prepared for children planning stops to visit tourist attractions they know about; and also for lots of discussions about children's own holidays along our two major highways.*

9 Hot chips

The cook at a school camp is working out his food order for the next month. He likes to make chips and knows that they are a favourite with most children. He calculates that he will need 49 kilograms of potatoes to feed everyone. When he goes to the store to buy the potatoes he finds that they are already packed and come in either 3-kg or 5-kg bags. He does not want to buy any more than 49 kilograms. How can he get the exact amount that he needs?

Curriculum links

This would be a good activity to do just before children go on a school camp. The activity could lead on to other investigations, for example: How many chips can be made from one potato? How many potatoes are there in 49 kilograms? How much would this many potatoes cost? How long does it take to cook chips? People's favourite ways to eat potatoes etc. This shows the possibilities for links with mass, money, time and graphing. We are sure you can think of many more.

DISCUSSING AND SOLVING THE PROBLEM

Most children find it hard to visualise 49 kilograms of potatoes. We showed our groups a one-kilogram bag and counted the number of potatoes in it so that they would gain a better understanding of the amount involved. This generated much discussion about how many potatoes there would be in 49 kilograms and provided an excellent opportunity for some estimation.

Once you are satisfied that the children understand the question, set them to work in groups to find some answers. Many groups we worked with tried initially to see if they could buy the potatoes all in 3-kg bags or all in 5-kg bags. When they found that they couldn't, they used trial and error to work it out and were satisfied when they found one answer. To reach a total of 49 kilograms, one group we watched approached the problem in a systematic way by making a table like the one opposite.

By the time they had finished they found three possible solutions and knew that they had found them all.

The groups who worked on a trial-and-error basis had difficulty in finding more than one solution.

We have 5-kg bags	We still need	3-kg bags
1 (= 5 kg)	44 kg	can't do
2 (= 10 kg)	39 kg	13 (= 49 kg)
3 (= 15 kg)	34 kg	can't do
4 (= 20 kg)	29 kg	can't do
5 (= 25 kg)	24 kg	8 (= 49 kg)
6 (= 30 kg)	19 kg	can't do
7 (= 35 kg)	14 kg	can't do
8 (= 40 kg)	9 kg	3 (= 49 kg)
9 (= 45 kg)	4 kg	can't do

BUILDING ON THE ACTIVITY

❑ When the children have finished, let each group tell the others how they worked out their answer. If no groups have done it systematically, do it together on the chalkboard. You can start with the 5-kg bags or the 3-kg bags.

49 Kg potatoes

5 kg
5 kg
5 kg
5 kg
5 kg
5 kg
5 kg
5 kg
3 kg
3 kg
3 kg
_49 kg_

5k bags

3 kg
3 kg
3 kg
3 kg
3 kg
3 kg
3 kg
5 kg
5 kg
5 kg
5 kg
_49 kg_

Jaimee Jeal

❑ Present the groups with a similar problem and ask them to work it out by making a table like the one you have on the chalkboard. A similar problem could be 67 kilograms of potatoes available in either 7-kg or 3-kg bags.

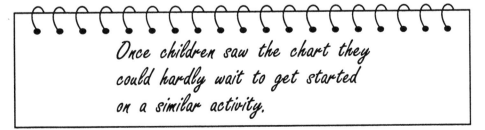

Once children saw the chart they could hardly wait to get started on a similar activity.

Building fences

How many fence posts do you need to build 100 metres of fence if the posts are 10 metres apart?

Curriculum links

This question looks simple. In fact, you will find that the students will tell you that the answer is 10 posts and will then dismiss the problem. But if you insist that they give you some proof for their answer, you will find that the children come up with all sorts of different ways of modelling it and their solutions can lead to exciting discoveries in perimeter, length and shape.

DISCUSSING AND SOLVING THE PROBLEM

You will find that after the children have read the problem silently and out loud, they will not even pause to make sure they fully understand the question, but will be eager to tell you an answer immediately. Let them tell you their answers, but then stop them and have one or two children explain the problem in their own words. Now challenge those children who gave immediate answers to find a way to prove their answer.

Once the children have decided how they are going to prove their answer, give them the chance to tell others their strategy. You will probably find that most will choose to make a diagram like the following:

Having done this, they can see by counting that 11 posts are needed. Make sure the children check that they do have 100 metres of fencing. Choose some children to share the reasons for the initial answers being wrong.

Now challenge the children to make 100 metres of fencing with only 10 posts placed equal distances apart. Give groups time to talk about this. Make sure you provide groups with rods, sticks, pencils and string etc. to help them model it.

We found that most children made or drew circular or rectangular fences. Below are examples of some possibilities.

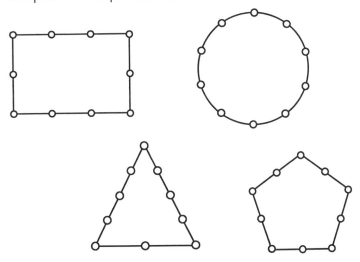

BUILDING ON THE ACTIVITY

❑ Have children suggest reasons for why these shapes use only 10 posts. (This is because only one post is used where the fence joins.)

❑ Let the children investigate other shapes that can be made with 10 posts.

❑ Have children investigate shapes that cannot be made with 10 posts, e.g. a square, a regular diamond, and try to explain why. They should be able to see that once the 4 corner posts are in place, then the remaining 6 posts cannot be distributed equally along the 4 sides.

❑ Some children may like to investigate how many posts are needed to make a square paddock.

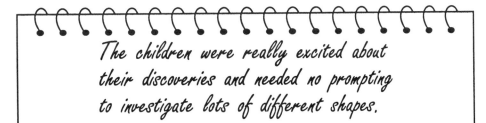

The children were really excited about their discoveries and needed no prompting to investigate lots of different shapes.

11 Football jumpers

When the manager of the local football team was very annoyed to see that they had no numbers on the back. He sent them back to the factory straight away. But the factory could only supply four digits: 1, 2, 5 and 7. Could they use these to make enough different numbers (of less than 100) so that a set of 18 jumpers could be ready for the first match?

Curriculum links

Children usually have little difficulty understanding the problem they are being asked to solve. They readily come up with different ways of finding numbers that can be made from the four digits available. The teacher's main task in this activity is to encourage them to generate numbers in an orderly way so that all possible numbers are found. This activity provides valuable practice in place value concepts and produces some interesting number patterns for the children to talk about.

DISCUSSING AND SOLVING THE PROBLEM

Ask the children to read through the problem silently and invite some children to explain to the rest of the class what it is asking them to find out (i.e. can they make at least 18 one- or two-digit numbers using 1, 2, 5 and 7?).

Put the children in groups and ask them to talk about how they can find the answer. Most groups come up with more than one strategy and are keen to start work. Let them start compiling their list of numbers before you interrupt them.

- Some groups just like to use pen and paper to write down the numbers as they make them up in their heads.
- Others like to write the four given digits on separate cards and shuffle these round to make numbers, with one person recording the numbers made.
- A more cumbersome variation of this is for children to make sets of each of the four digits using small cards and to arrange these on their desks to display their set of numbers, as shown opposite.

1	1 1	1 2	1 5	1 7
2	2 1	2 2	2 5	2 7
5	5 1	5 2	5 5	5 7
7	7 1	7 2	7 5	7 7

- Some groups we worked with asked for a 100 square and worked through it, circling all 20 numbers that could be made from combinations of 1, 2, 5 and 7. (You will find a 100 square on page 105 to copy for this purpose.)

Check each of the groups as they are working to see which ones are using a method that will generate all of the possible numbers in some sort of order, and which groups are producing numbers at random. Stop the class at this stage for a share time and ask one member from each group to explain what they are doing. Groups that are using inefficient or random methods usually take this opportunity to try a new method.

When the groups have finished their work, have another share time to let them compare answers with the other groups and to talk about the number patterns they found as they were working.

BUILDING ON THE ACTIVITY

❑ Let the children investigate what would happen if the factory only had 0, 2, 5 and 7 to make numbers with. What difference does the zero make?

❑ Let the children investigate how many numbers (of less than 100) can be made from any five given digits and then from six digits. Can they predict how many numbers can be made with seven digits?

❑ If the factory can supply the digits 0, 1, 2, 3, 4, 5, 7, 8 and 9, but no 6's, how many of the numbers between 1 and 100 would not be able to be made? Give the children a 100 square to help them work this out.

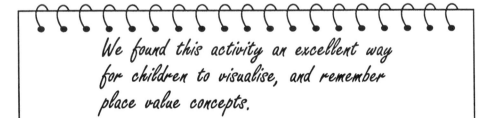

We found this activity an excellent way for children to visualise, and remember place value concepts.

12 Spending money

You have been given $5 to spend at the souvenir shop. You want to buy something that you can keep as a reminder of your visit as well as something to give to your parents when you get home. After looking around the shop you can see some suitable items, but you cannot decide which of these to buy. The items you are interested in are:

    silver plated spoons–$2.50 a pair
    writing pads–$1.50 each
    decorated pencils–$1.00 for 3
    fancy fridge magnets–50 cents each

Finally you make up your mind. When you leave the shop you have spent all your money. What might you have bought?

Curriculum links

This scenario often arises on a school trip and it takes forever for some children to make their purchases. Many children have great difficulty working out what they can buy for their money, especially when there are a few choices involved. This problem will help them to see that there are many different combinations of goods that they could buy for their $5. We found that this problem created lots of heated discussion amongst groups about what each person would choose, and led to a class discussion about value for money.

DISCUSSING AND SOLVING THE PROBLEM

This is quite an easy problem to understand, so after reading it and having some children explain it in their own words, let the groups begin work. Have some play money available and plenty of paper so groups can choose the material they want to work with. Listen to groups as they start and make sure that they all understand that the whole $5 has to be spent, that the spoons must be bought as a pair and the pencils in groups of 3.

Although this task is easy to understand it is not so easy to work out, as you will soon see. We found that most groups chose to write down their possibilities and at the start this worked well. However, as they progressed they became very confused because they could not remember the combinations of goods they had chosen and much time was spent checking this. Frustration started to set in. If this happens in your class, stop the groups working and discuss ways of making the task easier to record.

After initial frustration, two of our groups had realised they needed to find the possibilities systematically and had started by first recording the six possible combinations that went with buying the spoons.

These are:

2 sets of spoons
1 set of spoons + 1 writing pad + 1 set of pencils
1 set of spoons + 1 writing pad + 2 magnets
1 set of spoons + 5 magnets
1 set of spoons + 2 sets of pencils + 1 magnet
1 set of spoons + 1 set of pencils + 3 magnets

After they completed this, they then started with the writing pad and recorded the eight possible combinations. The pencils came next with five possibilities, and lastly the magnets with the only possible combination being 10 magnets. Once children realise that they can record systematically, let them go back to the task. When most groups have finished, let them show the others how they recorded all twenty possibilities.

BUILDING ON THE ACTIVITY

❑ Once all combinations have been found, ask each group to decide which of the twenty possibilities it would choose. Be prepared for disagreement! Group members find it really difficult to agree on this. However, the talk that arises focuses on whether value for money is getting the most items or getting quality items. When groups present their final decision, ask them to say why they chose that option.

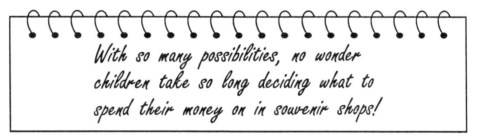

With so many possibilities, no wonder children take so long deciding what to spend their money on in souvenir shops!

13 | Shop display

The manager of a paint store wanted to display a new wash'n'wear super acrylic paint in the centre of his store. He decided to make a square pyramid with cans of paint. If he uses six cans of paint for the width of the base, how many cans of paint will he need altogether for the pyramid?

Curriculum links

This problem provides a good combination of shape and number concepts. The children enjoy constructing the square pyramid (and other shapes) and get valuable practice in dealing with square numbers. They are very surprised to see the total number of cans needed to build the pyramid.

DISCUSSING AND SOLVING THE PROBLEM

After they have read the problem, some children will be uncertain what to do because they are not exactly sure what a square pyramid looks like. Choose some children to explain what the square pyramid would look like (it will have a square base and four triangular sides). Let some children draw one on the chalkboard for others to see. It would also be a good idea to supply a model for the children to look at. Explain that the store manager is going to make each side of the base six cans wide. Do not ask for children to start building a pyramid at this stage as it makes the task too easy.

Put the children in groups and tell them that there are cubes/blocks/tins available to help them if they wish to use them. (You should have about 100 identical stackable objects ready for each group to use.) Let the children start work and watch what strategies each group adopts.

- Some will not want to use blocks and will be able to roughly sketch the pyramid and calculate the answer from this by adding together the number of cans in each layer (i.e. $36 + 25 + 16 + 9 + 4 + 1 = 91$).
- Other groups will make a sketch but not realise that the pyramid must be solid and built up in layers. These groups try to count the number of cans on one side of the pyramid so they can multiply this by four, but they lose track

because they do not know what to do with the corner cans that belong to two sides. Suggest to any groups who fall into this trap that they try building the pyramid with blocks.

■ Other groups will build a square pyramid with a 6 × 6 base, followed by a 5 × 5 layer, a 4 × 4 layer, a 3 × 3 layer, a 2 × 2 layer and a single can on the top.

The groups who record how many cans there are in each layer as they go, reach the correct answer first. Those groups who build the entire pyramid before they start any counting, sometimes get as confused as the groups who try to count the cans on each of the sides. When all the groups have reached an answer (or the end of their tether!), let one representative from each group report to the class about what method the group used and how they worked out their answer.

BUILDING ON THE ACTIVITY

❑ Those children who got side-tracked by using poor strategies are usually very eager to have another go.

Ask the children to find how many cans are needed for four-, five- and seven-sided pyramids. Some children will be able to work these out by pen and paper methods using the sequence of square numbers they found in the six-can pyramid. Others will need to build some or all of these to find the answer. It is important to let the children choose their own method—both methods provide valuable learning opportunities.

❑ For children who are really keen to continue, let them investigate the number of cans needed for triangular pyramids (or any other 3-D shape they choose).

> *This can be a very noisy activity!*
> *It would be a good idea to work on*
> *a carpeted area using foam blocks.*

14 Parking fees

You need to park your car from 9:15 a.m. until 12:45 p.m. Which of these two car-parks would you choose to park your car in?

PAT'S CAR-PARK
$4.00 - 1st hour
$2.50 - each additional hour or part of the hour
MAXIMUM - $15.00

PAM'S CAR-PARK
1st hour - FREE
2nd hour - $3.00
$1.50 for each additional 15 minutes

Curriculum links

Money and time are linked in this activity. Most children will know that charges are made for car-parking but may not have looked closely at the issue. This is a great activity to do before an excursion to a large city centre. It alerts children to the costs involved in parking and gives them a reason for collecting data during the excursion.

DISCUSSING AND SOLVING THE PROBLEM

Before showing this problem to the class, tell them about your 'trip' to the city and how it took you 30 minutes to find a car-park and when you did it cost a small fortune! Allow children to relate similar experiences. Then show them the problem. Give them time to read it silently and choose a couple of children to read it out loud. Ask two or three children to restate the problem in their own words. Ask the children to say which car-park looks cheaper at first sight (without working it out) and then tell the groups to find out which is actually cheaper.

Mostly, children will say that the second one looks cheaper because the first hour is free. The groups we worked with found this problem fairly easy to understand and required little or no help at this early stage. One group requested a clock with moveable hands to assist them working out how many lots of 15 minutes there were from 11:15 a.m. until 12:45 p.m.

As the groups continued working we realised that some of them were unsure of the meaning of the word 'additional', so we stopped them and discussed this as it related to the problem. Our groups finished about the same time so they returned to the floor where we allowed each group to tell how they worked out the two car-park charges. All groups found that the cost at the first park would be $11.50 and at the second it would be $12.00.

$4.00 – 1st hrs
$2.50 – 2nd hrs
$2.50 – 3rd hrs
$2.50 – ½ hrs
––––––––––––
$11.50

Free – 1st hrs
$3.00 – 2nd hrs
$6.00 – 3rd hrs
$3.00 – ½ hrs
––––––––––––
$12.00

3 and a ½ hours total

chris

BUILDING ON THE ACTIVITY

❑ Ask the groups to work out how long they would have to stay at the first car-park to get the benefit of the $15.00 maximum charge and how long they could stay at the second car-park for $15.00.

❑ Now ask them to compare the two parks hour by hour over a 5-hour period and to recommend which one we should park at if we wanted to visit the city for 1 hour, 2 hours, 3 hours, 4 hours or 5 hours.

❑ If you are going on an excursion to a large city centre, have the children write down any car-parking charges that they see. They could even collect the charges from some parking meters. Back at school, work out comparative prices for each hour and present the findings to the rest of the class.

❑ Discuss whether it is cheaper to use another form of transport to travel to the city. What are the advantages and disadvantages?

For weeks after this activity children kept bringing in new car-park charges that they or their parents had found.

The government of Ruritangia had decided that the country needed a new flag. They had found out that $5/8$ of the politicians preferred blue, $1/4$ liked yellow and $1/8$ wanted the colour to be red. So they decided that the flag would be $5/8$ blue, $1/4$ yellow and $1/8$ red, but they couldn't agree on a design. Can you design a new flag for Ruritangia?

Curriculum links

Children really enjoy this activity. It is an excellent way for children to develop their understanding of fractions and also provides experience with conservation of area, shape and pattern. Unless your class has had plenty of experience at working independently, it is best to treat this lesson in two stages, making sure that all children are given enough guidance to complete each stage successfully.

DISCUSSING AND SOLVING THE PROBLEM

For this activity it is best to have the children in groups from the outset. Give each child a copy of page 101 as they are reading through the problem on the chalkboard. Tell the children to discuss in groups what they are being asked to do and how they can use the sheet to help them. The children are usually keen to have a go at designing a new flag and can see that the grid on the sheet can help them mark off the fractions needed for each colour. However, many are not confident of doing this. Ask these groups to try to work out how to find $1/4$, $1/8$ and $5/8$ of their flag and to rule along the grid lines to mark off each of these fractions.

Move about the room and watch how the children go about solving this problem. Some will use area and some will use the number of squares on the grid. At share time, try to make sure both of these methods are demonstrated.

■ The children who use number will have counted that there are 80 squares on the grid and worked out that $1/4$ of these is ($80 \div 4 =$) 20 squares, $1/8$ is ($80 \div 8 =$) 10 squares and therefore $5/8$ is ($10 \times 5 =$) 50 squares.

■ The children who use area are usually less confident with fractions. They fold or rule the grid into four equal parts to find the $1/4$. Then they realise that if they divide each quarter into two, they have made 8 equal pieces and each of these is $1/8$ of the flag. They can also see that the $1/4$ is the same size as $2/8$. After they have marked off the $1/4$ and $1/8$ they check to see what is left and realise that five of the $1/8$ pieces are left and this is the $5/8$ they need for the other fraction.

When all the children have marked off the three fractions on their flag, it is time to move on to designing the new flag. One way to go about this is to have the children working in pairs. On one sheet they colour in each of the fractions the correct colour, then cut the flag into small squares of colour by cutting along the grid lines. Then they use their second sheet as a base or outline on which they can try out different arrangements of their squares of colour. When they are happy with their design, they can paste the squares of colour into position on the second sheet.

Some children ask if they can cut some of their coloured squares diagonally to make triangles or into some other smaller shape. Children who do this usually end up with a much more intricate design. The completed flags make a wonderfully colourful display!

BUILDING ON THE ACTIVITY

❑ Let the children investigate flags of the world. Choose some of the simpler geometric designs and ask the children to work out what fraction of the flag is a particular colour. For example: What fraction of the Italian flag is green? What fraction of the Mauritian flag is yellow? What fraction of the Colombian flag is blue?

❑ Investigate some of the more complex designs (Sudan, Finland, Kuwait, Thailand) by copying them on to grid paper (or use the grid on page 101) and counting how many squares of each colour there are to find out what fraction of the flag each colour is.

It is important to let children use their own method of finding the fractions — they choose the way they understand best and this provides the teacher with guidance for future lesson planning.

16 | **Business sense**

Tim is starting his own regular weekly cleaning service and decides to begin slowly and build up customers as he goes. He works out a plan where he will begin with one customer in the first week and add two new jobs a week until he has 19 customers per week. If everything goes to plan, how many weeks will it take Tim to get to this stage and how many cleaning jobs will he have done in this time?

Curriculum links

Identifying the pattern, counting by twos and addition are all part of this problem. It is also interesting to discuss Tim's business plan. What factors could assist or hinder his plan?

DISCUSSING AND SOLVING THE PROBLEM

week	Jobs
1	1
2	3
3	5
4	7
5	9
6	11
7	13
8	15
9	+17
10	19
	100

Adam B

Some children find it difficult to visualise this type of cumulative pattern. Therefore, it is important to spend time discussing what will actually happen each week so that children have a picture in their minds. Before groups start working, focus on the two questions asked and make sure the children can tell you in their own words what they have to find out.

While the groups are working it is interesting to watch some of the methods that the children use. Lots of groups use pen and paper in various ways, others use counters to represent the customers, some use calculators and others use a combination of these methods.

- One group who used calculators started by showing the number of customers for each week, i.e. 1, 3, 5, 7, 9, 11 etc. until they reached 19. At this point they looked at the question again and realised they had not answered it. They repeated the task, keeping count of the number of weeks and adding each number to the previous number progressively so that they arrived at the answer of 100 cleaning jobs over 10 weeks.
- A group using pen and paper arrived at this same answer but they listed the pattern first, i.e. 1, 3, 5, 7, 9, 11, 13, 15, 17, 19, so that they could count the weeks and then added these numbers together.

Quite a few groups used calculators to add the numbers together or to check their addition. After the groups have finished, allow them time to tell the others how they did the task and then ask children to comment on Tim's business plan.

46

Most children in our groups simply accepted that the plan would work and very few thought about the circumstances that could stop it succeeding. In the next section we describe how we continued this.

BUILDING ON THE ACTIVITY

❑ We asked each group to list all the things that might stop Tim from adding two new customers a week, e.g. a previous customer decides to pull out, no new customers apply etc. We also asked groups to decide what they would do if more than the planned two new customers wanted cleaning in any week. When the groups reported their decisions, all had decided that they could not afford to be choosy about customers and that they should take the work when it was available. Some groups had also looked at the possibility of hiring extra staff if there were so many new customers that Tim could not cope by himself. It was good to develop this activity along these lines so that the children could appreciate that the initial situation described, was artificial.

❑ It would also be interesting to extend the pattern to twenty weeks, i.e. 21, 23, 25, 27, 29, 31, 33, 35, 37, 39, and work out how many jobs would have been done altogether. If you ask children to guess, most would say '200' because they had doubled 100, when in fact if they work it out, they find the answer is 400.

Try to relate situations to real life wherever possible.

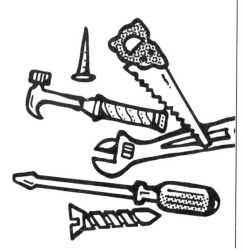

17 Make one metre

Francesca wanted a piece of wood one metre long to nail along the edge of the shelf in her cubby house so that her books wouldn't fall off. She looked under the house and in her father's workshop, but could not find any. When her father came home from work she asked him to help. He found ten smaller pieces that, when nailed together, would make exactly one metre. Each of the ten pieces was a different length. One of the pieces was 3 centimetres long and another was 17 centimetres long. Can you work out what the lengths of the other eight pieces were?

Curriculum links

This activity offers a great opportunity to 'play around' with numbers. Children are encouraged to not only add numbers but to search for number patterns. The link with measurement is made through the centimetre being used as the unit. Children do need to make use of the fact that 100 centimetres equals one metre.

DISCUSSING AND SOLVING THE PROBLEM

At first, most children don't see this as a number problem. They find it hard to see through the measurement story to get to the main problem. After an initial reading it may be best to let groups discuss it to work out what they actually have to do and then share their thoughts. This way you will be able to check if they have in fact understood the task and to help groups who haven't. Then let groups start work.

Most groups will begin using trial and error, starting with 3 and 17 and choosing eight more numbers and then adding them up. One group we watched said that 'since 3 and 17 makes 20, we need to look for eight different numbers to total 80'. Unless a group finds a solution by accident, it is unlikely that groups will solve it without further help. You will find that children will start to say things like, 'Is it possible? Can you give us a clue?'.

This is the time to call them together again and share what each group has done to try and find a pattern. If no group focuses on the pattern, tell the children that the fact that 3 and 17 add up to 20 has something to do with the answer. Ask them how many 20's there are in 100 and what other pairs of numbers add up to 20. Show a few of these on the chalkboard, for example 1 and 19, 2 and 18 etc. and then let the groups do the rest. They will see that there are ten pairs of numbers (1 and 19, 2 and 18, 3 and 17, 4 and 16, 5 and 15,

$$\begin{matrix} 3 \\ + \\ 17 \end{matrix} = 20cm$$

$$\begin{matrix} 16 \\ + \\ 4 \end{matrix} = 20cm$$

$$\begin{matrix} 15 \\ + \\ 5 \end{matrix} = 20cm$$

$$\begin{matrix} 18 \\ + \\ 2 \end{matrix} = 20cm$$

$$\begin{matrix} 13 \\ + \\ 7 \end{matrix} = 20cm \quad \text{Allanna}$$

6 and 14, 7 and 13, 8 and 12, 9 and 11, 10 and 10), each of which add up to 20. Any five of these pairs will add up to 100. They cannot use 10 and 10 because each piece of wood was a different length and they must use 3 and 17 as stated in the story.

Give groups time to choose the lengths of wood they think Francesca's father found and then share their choices with the others.

BUILDING ON THE ACTIVITY

❏ Provide lengths of paper or card and let groups cut them to the lengths they have chosen to see if, when put together, it does equal one metre. Have each group place their one metre next to the other so that all groups can see the different ways to make 100 centimetres. It is a good idea to make a class chart for display which shows all the possibilities.

❏ Children can further investigate this set of numbers by seeing if it is possible to make 100 with only odd numbers or only even numbers.

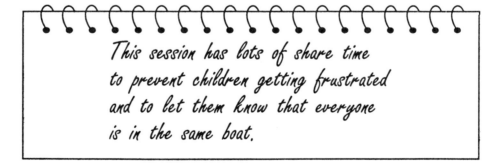

This session has lots of share time to prevent children getting frustrated and to let them know that everyone is in the same boat.

18 Theatre tickets

Our local secondary college was giving its annual performance. The theatre had 100 seats. Opening-night was a sell-out—all 100 seats were taken. They raised $98. The second night was also a sell-out, but this time they raised $132.50. The tickets were sold at $2 for adults and 50 cents for children. When the secretary was checking the takings, she couldn't work out why more money was collected on the second night when the same number of seats were sold for both performances. Can you work out the reason for this?

Curriculum links

This task involves children in working with doubling and halving amounts of money. It also looks at strategies for increasing the amount of money taken.

DISCUSSING AND SOLVING THE PROBLEM

Even after the children have read this silently and then out loud, you will need much class discussion to clarify the information and the task. Many children will have the same 'problem' as the secretary—they won't understand how more money can be raised on the second night when exactly the same number of tickets have been sold.

We suggest that you put children in groups to work out reasons why the takings on the two nights are different. You will find they come up with reasons such as: the ticket sellers didn't give the right change; they sold more tickets on the second night; they sold more $2 seats on the second night; more adults came on the second night. Share these ideas and together with the children, talk about and eliminate incorrect and unlikely possibilities. It should become obvious to the children that only the last two ideas (which are actually the same) are likely.

Once the children have reached this stage, set groups to work to find how many adult and children's tickets were sold for each performance. It is a good idea to start this as a class by saying, 'We know there are 100 seats. Let's assume that we have 50 adults and 50 children. Work out how much money this would raise.' Do this on the chalkboard so the children can see that there would be $100 for the adult tickets and $25 for the children's tickets. That is, $125 in total.

Now say, 'But they only took $98. What can we do to lower the amount of $125 we got from our first try?'. Listen to the children's suggestions and focus on those that recommend less than 50 adults and more than 50 children buying tickets. Once the children understand what they have to do, let them work as groups. You will find some groups will do this purely by trial and error, others will use the information they have found from 50 adults/50 children and expand on it. A group we watched insisted on working out every combination of adults and children from 50/50 until they reached the combination of 32 adults and 68 children making $98.

When most groups have the answer, share the ways they worked it out and praise the groups who used the initial information effectively.

Now ask the groups to build on this information to work out how many adults and children attended the second performance. We found that although this took time, all groups were confident they knew how to find the answer (55 adults and 45 children) and were keen to share this with the rest of the class.

BUILDING ON THE ACTIVITY

❑ Look at ways of increasing the amount of money taken for each performance. What is the maximum/minimum amount of money that can be raised from one performance?

❑ Find out how seats are priced at some of your local theatres — are the prices the same for everyone, or is the price based on the position of the seat?

> When children are doing this task, watch to see how they double their numbers. Do they multiply by 2 or add the numbers together? This information is useful for evaluation records.

19 Duty rosters

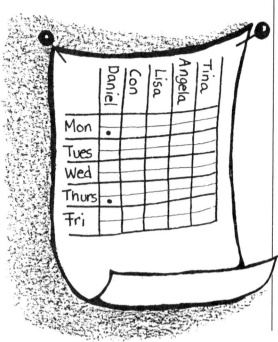

Kim, the manager of the university canteen is working out the duty roster for the following week. She has five people to allocate time to and each person works for one day. Each of the five people have other commitments which limit when they can work, and so they put in requests for certain times. Kim takes note of their requests, which are as follows:

- Daniel can only work Monday and Thursday afternoons.
- Lisa wants to work all one day.
- Con can only work in the mornings.
- Angela wants to work two days in a row.
- Tina wants to work one morning and one afternoon.
- Angela and Con cannot work on the same day.

Can you help Kim do the duty roster to suit everyone's request?

Curriculum links

Duty rosters and timetables are an integral part of many of our activities. It is important that children learn how to organise and read information on tables or charts. This activity allows children to make a visual representation of a duty roster and see that there are various ways of solving the problem.

DISCUSSING AND SOLVING THE PROBLEM

This particular activity arose from one lunch-time when the lunches from the canteen didn't arrive on time and the children wanted to know why. When we inquired, we found that one person who was rostered had not turned up. Some of the children were not sure what a roster was or how it worked, so we decided to do some rosters of our own.

All the children found this task fairly easy to understand and showed this by being able to tell us in their own words what they had to do. Before the groups got started we asked them to talk about how they were going to approach the task. All groups said they would make a chart, something like a timetable, which showed mornings and afternoons for one week. When they started work, the charts varied in format from group to group but all were quite suitable. We asked each group to do a good copy for presentation purposes. When most groups were nearing the end of this task, we stopped all of them and told them that there was more than one solution to this problem. We challenged each group to find another way of organising the duty roster so that it still satisfied everyone's requirements.

Before they started to do this, we said we had noticed that when working on their first roster nearly every group had crossed out names a lot before arriving at their final roster. We asked children to think about how they could do their next roster and avoid this messy crossing-out of names. Very quickly, children responded that they could put the names on pieces of paper and move them around until they were happy with the roster. We asked all groups to do this when planning the second roster. If your groups do not suggest this, then tell them and ask them to try it. Again, when the rosters were complete, we had each group do a good copy.

Our share time focused on the presentation of possible rosters. Our groups presented four variations. We also discussed the order in which each group had filled in the names, e.g. Daniel's name first, Lisa's name second but with a choice of 3 days etc. The finished rosters were displayed on the backboard.

BUILDING ON THE ACTIVITY

❑ Look at your school timetables, particularly those for specialist classes such as art, library, physical education etc. and talk about how classes are allocated certain times. What things are considered when these times are planned?

❑ Give each group a copy of the daily timetables on page 102 and ask them to plan timetables for each of the four grades for art, library, drama and physical education. This is quite a difficult activity unless children follow a pattern. Again, it is a good idea to have the subject names written on pieces of paper so they can be moved around until they are satisfactory.

Discuss the pattern with the children. What happens if you do not follow this pattern?

> *The children were astounded at how tricky it was to plan timetables. They were immediately more understanding of the fact that their specialist lessons were not at all the times they would wish them to be.*

Wheeling and dealing

Louis bought a pair of roller blades at a garage sale for $30 and sold them to his cousin the next day for $40. That night he thought about the fun he could have had with the roller blades and wished he hadn't sold them. So the next day he bought them back from his cousin for $50. While roller-blading later that day he had a nasty fall and decided that it would be a good idea to sell them again. He took them to the local recycling shop where the manager paid him $60. Did Louis make money, lose money, or break even on the deal?

Curriculum links

It is essential that children have experience with problems like this. So often people lose money on deals because they cannot think them through. It is easy to become confused if you don't look at the parts of this problem in order. This activity has links with money and mental arithmetic. We suggest you have plenty of play money available to use when needed. Strips of paper each representing $10 would be suitable.

DISCUSSING AND SOLVING THE PROBLEM

You will probably find the children will want to give their opinion almost immediately after they have read this problem. If this happens, it is better to let them do this before you discuss the problem further. Even record their opinions in three columns on the chalkboard so they can look back later to see if they changed their mind.

Now focus the children's attention on the problem again and make sure they all know what they have to do before joining their groups. Tell everyone that their group must first discuss the problem before deciding what, if anything, they will use to work it out. We found this problem produced lots and lots of talk amongst groups—much of it bordering on argument! However, because the members of each group had to reach agreement, the discussion is vital.

After a while, stop the groups and ask them to share with other groups how they were going about solving the problem. Of our groups, none had thought of any method other than discussion, but now suggested the possibility of using play money to act it out. All the groups thought this sounded like a good idea and collected the play money which we had ready. It was interesting to watch how the groups worked now. If anything, the money caused more arguments than before because they started with only $30, and therefore lost track when they had to pay $50 to get the roller blades back as they didn't have this amount of money.

Again, stop the groups and have them all come out to the floor—it is time to provide a clue. Talk about how most people, when going to buy something, begin with more money in their wallet than they need. For example, if one of us was going to buy the roller blades, it would be likely that we would have at least $50 in our wallet. After all the buying and selling processes are complete, it would be easy to see how much we had made or lost by comparing the amount left in our wallet with the amount we had started with. Suggest that each group should decide on an amount of money no less than $50 to have at the start. It did not take long from this point for our groups to use the play money to solve the problem and work out that they would make $20 on the deal.

We finished this part of our lesson by comparing children's initial opinions with the end result.

BUILDING ON THE ACTIVITY

❑ Make up a similar problem for children to solve or use the same scenario and change the amounts of money, e.g. buy for $50, sell for $40, buy for $50 and sell for $70.

❑ Ask groups to make up their own money problem based on this one, but to do it so the dealer breaks even.

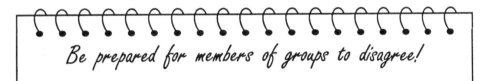

Be prepared for members of groups to disagree!

21 Popular letters

If you were going to play Hangman or Wheel of Fortune you can improve your chance of winning by knowing which letters are used more often than others to make words. Work out a way to check this. Which letters would help you win Hangman or Wheel of Fortune?

Curriculum links

When playing the above games, most children randomly select or guess letters without realising that some letters occur more frequently than others. This activity will give them a strategy for increasing their chances of choosing the correct letters early in a game. By correct placement of these letters early, they have more chance of completing words or phrases. This activity links with statistics through probability theory and frequency distribution charts.

DISCUSSING AND SOLVING THE PROBLEM

What better way to start this activity than to play two or three class games of Hangman. Do this before children are shown the task. After you have finished the games, leave the words on the chalkboard and ask, 'Which letter(s) occurred most often in these words?'. Discuss this and talk about other situations where it would be useful to know which letters occur frequently, e.g. games such as Wheel of Fortune, Scrabble, and when doing crosswords.

Now show the task to the children and ask them to read it silently. Choose a few children to read it out loud and then ask other class members to suggest ways of checking which letters are used most frequently. In our groups quite a few children said there was no need to check as the vowels are always used more than the consonants (even if this didn't happen in the class Hangman game!). Most children generally suggest counting letters from a page of writing. After all the children's ideas have been given, let them join their groups to talk about the strategies and decide which one their group will try.

Before the groups start, ask each to guess the five letters which they think will occur most frequently and write these on the chalkboard. You can compare their findings with these later. Make sure you have plenty of books and newspapers available. It is fascinating to watch the ways in which different groups collect this information. Some rule blank paper with separate columns for each letter and use tally marks; some start by writing the letters in groups each time they occur, but soon realise they need to be more systematic; some use a tick system. All are a form of frequency distribution.

If some groups are struggling with recording the information, stop everyone and show the work of the groups who have started successfully. This should give them some clues. When the children have completed this task and found the letters that occur most frequently, write them on the board next to each group's guess. The results will vary from group to group, but they would be likely to find that E, T, A, O and N are used often. On the other hand, you should not find Q, Z, K, X and J occurring very often.

Spend some of the share time looking at the way groups recorded the information and discussing which was most effective. You could finish with a game of either Hangman or Wheel of Fortune and test your findings.

BUILDING ON THE ACTIVITY

❏ Have each group turn their frequency distribution chart into a graph. Let them decide how they are going to do this, i.e. what type of graph they will use. When the graphs are finished, display them and discuss which shows the information most effectively.

❏ Look more closely at the way the information was recorded on the frequency charts. Who used tally marks (e.g. ┼┼┼) to keep count? Let all the children practise keeping a tally by doing a car survey, a head count etc.

Use this activity as a starting point to develop children's knowledge of letter patterns.

22 | Millionaire

A 21 year old woman won $1 000 000 in a lottery. She had no idea what she should do with the money, never having had that much before. She decided to work out how long the money would last if she spent $100 each day. Can you help her work it out? How old would she be when she has spent it all?

Curriculum links

It is hard for the majority of children (and adults!) to imagine $1 000 000 and appreciate what can be done with such a large sum of money. This activity helps children to see just how much $1 000 000 is. The mathematics in this activity is not all that difficult but the large numbers are off-putting for many children. The hard part is identifying how to work this out, i.e. what mathematical processes to use. We suggest you encourage children to estimate first and then let them use calculators to confirm their estimate.

DISCUSSING AND SOLVING THE PROBLEM

Before showing this problem to the class, ask them to imagine winning one million dollars in a lottery and to think about what they would do with it. Give each child a strip of paper and ask them to write a sentence, telling what they would do. Put these strips of paper on the board with Blu-Tack for everyone to see and discuss if the plans are possible.

After the discussion, show the problem to the class, let them read it quietly and out loud and then ask each group to talk about how they would work out the first part of the problem. Stress that you only want them to decide how they are going to do the problem, not to actually do it.

We followed this up with a share time to inform the other groups of the chosen strategies and found this very enlightening. We had imagined that most groups would simply want to divide $1 000 000 by 100. However, some of the suggestions were:

- repeatedly subtracting $100 from $1 000 000 and keeping count of how many times you do it;

- working out how much money you would spend in one year, two years etc. and using this information to solve the problem.
- working out how much money would be spent per week ($700), multiply this by 52 weeks and divide this into $1 000 000.

The groups were permitted to change their strategy after the share time if they wished. We had calculators available but asked that children estimate first and then use the calculator to confirm their estimate. It did not take long for groups to finish this part, some giving their answer in days (10 000 days) and others in years (a little more than 27 years). The group who was going to subtract $100 repeatedly, changed their strategy after the share time!

We then asked groups to work out the second part of the problem. This was easy for those groups who had calculated the first part in years, but took a little longer for those groups who had calculated in days. (The lottery winner would be 48 years old.)

BUILDING ON THE ACTIVITY

❑ As the children were working on the calculations, they commented on variations between groups in some of the results, e.g. one group worked out that $700 per week would be spent, which means $52 \times \$700$ equals $36 400 per year; another group based their calculation on $100 per day for 365 days, which is $36 500 per year; and another group based theirs on a 30-day month, which is $3000 per month and $36 000 per year.

As a class, we talked about the reasons why this happened and asked the children to say which method was the most accurate. We also looked at how the various methods affected the outcome and found that all methods gave a result between 27 and 28 years.

❑ Talk about whether spending $100 each day would be wise. Most children would see that this was not really practical. Now look back at the ways the children had initially said they would spend one million dollars and ask if anyone would like to change their mind. (Quite a few children in our groups did, especially those who had said they would never have to work again!)

We made a class chart titled 'How I Would Spend $1 000 000' with each child's name written on the left-hand side and their ideas beside it. We displayed this in the room. We also bought a lottery ticket!

Writing numbers

Emily's teacher had been talking about how big the number 1 000 000 is. He challenged the children to write down all the numbers from 1 to 1 000 000. Emily thought that it would be an easy thing to do. But after writing 28 905 digits her hand ached and she was sick of the whole thing. What number did Emily get up to?

Curriculum links

After you have cleared up the initial confusion about the distinction between digits and numbers, the children find this a fairly straight-forward problem. It provides them with excellent practice in dealing with place value, using calculators and operating with large numbers.

DISCUSSING AND SOLVING THE PROBLEM

After reading the problem, a number of children will be clearly confused because they are unsure about the difference between the words 'digit' and 'number'. Choose several children to explain what the problem is asking them to find out and if necessary, let some of these children demonstrate on the chalkboard the difference between numbers and digits (i.e. the number 104 has three digits 1, 0 and 4). Now ask the children to predict what number Emily reached and write some of these on the chalkboard. (The range is usually somewhere between 1 000 and 10 000.)

   Put the children into their working groups and offer each group a calculator and a 100 square to help them with their working out. (You can make copies of the 100 squares on page 105 for this purpose.) Let the groups start working and move around the room to observe how they devise a method of tackling the problem. Some groups we worked with used the 100 square and started counting the digits in one continuous addition process. Others realised that the numbers could be broken into groups according to how many digits they had, and this made the addition more manageable and easier to check for errors. If you still have groups just counting strings of digits after the first five minutes, stop the class for a share time so that the groups can compare methods and switch to a more efficient counting method if necessary.

The next problem the children meet is to work out how many numbers there are between, say, 10 and 99. Many will not be sure whether it is 89 or 90. If several groups are struggling with this, it may be wise to stop and work out the digits from 1 to 99 as a whole class on the chalkboard, e.g.

one-digit numbers (1–9)	9 numbers × 1 digit	= 9
two-digit numbers (10–99)	90 numbers × 2 digits	= 180
		189

Once the children have got this far, they usually have little trouble in continuing on to reach the final answer (7503). When the children have finished their calculations, choose one representative from each group to describe how the group reached their answer. Let the children continue the table on the chalkboard, e.g.

three-digit numbers (100–999)	900 numbers × 3 digits	= 2700
		+ 189
		2889
four-digit numbers (1000–9999)	9000 numbers × 4 digits	= 36 000

So the last number Emily wrote has to be less than 9999. She had written 2889 digits before she got to the four-digit numbers, so she wrote (28 905 − 2889 =) 26 016 digits as four-digit numbers. 26 016 digits will make 6504 four-digit numbers.

So Emily wrote:

9	one-digit numbers
90	two-digit numbers
900	three-digit numbers
+ 6504	four-digit numbers
7503	numbers.

BUILDING ON THE ACTIVITY

❏ Work out how many digits there are altogether in the numbers 1 to 1 000 000.

❏ If Emily wrote one digit each second, how long did she spend writing? How long would it have taken her to write all the numbers up to 1 000 000?

❏ Do you think you will live 1 000 000 days?

Once the children have mastered one of these six-digit problems their confidence increases enormously and, armed with a calculator, some feel mathematically invincible!

24 | Running race

The running track at the athletics club is circular. There are six red flags around the track, each the same distance apart. Yesterday, a runner was practising for the annual athletic carnival to be held next weekend. She took 30 seconds to get to the third flag. If she keeps running at the same speed, how long will it take her to run all the way around the track?

Curriculum links

This problem is similar to 'Building fences', but is made a little more complicated by the inclusion of the time factor. The problem looks simple but children need to draw a diagram or model the track to see where their error is. As in 'Building fences', this activity can lead to work with perimeter. It could also lead to activities associated with measuring and time.

DISCUSSING AND SOLVING THE PROBLEM

Let children start responding to this one straight away. You will probably find that most children come up with an answer of 60 seconds almost immediately and are convinced that they are correct. Tell them that 60 seconds is not the correct answer and let groups of children work out another possibility. We have found that most groups will now draw the circular track and the flags. (This is interesting to watch, particularly when groups try to position the flags equal distances apart!) Once the groups have made their drawing they can usually see quite easily that the runner would take 90 seconds. Ask each group to show their drawing or model and explain how the runner would take 90 seconds. Some groups might explain where they went wrong initially.

BUILDING ON THE ACTIVITY

❑ Take the children to a running track or oval and measure the distance around the boundary. Have the children place 'flags' equal distances apart, as in the problem. Let the groups work out how to do this, but make sure that you have trundle wheels and measuring tapes available. When the flags are positioned, decide on a starting point and time how long it takes for one child to run around the track. Work out how many seconds it would have taken this runner to reach the third flag. (You will have to assume that the speed is the same for the entire distance.) Compare this with the 30 seconds taken by the runner in the problem.

❑ You could also investigate the time splits for each flag by noting down the time as the child reaches each flag. Is the speed constant? Have children give reasons for their findings.

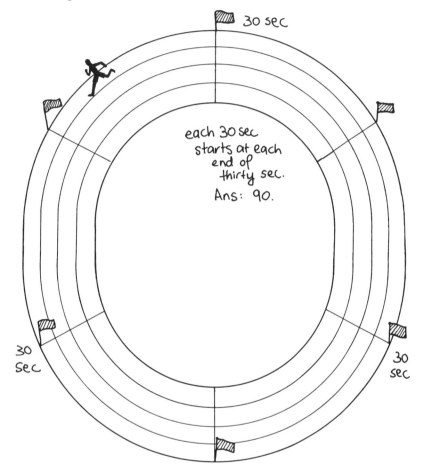

30 sec

each 30 sec
starts at each
end of
thirty sec.
Ans: 90.

30 sec

30 sec

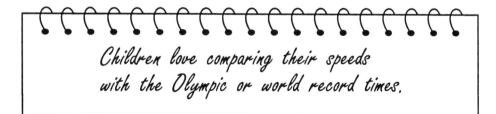

*Children love comparing their speeds
with the Olympic or world record times.*

25 Letter writing

Alice starts a chain letter and writes to five of her friends who each write to five of their friends, who each then write to five of their friends. How many letters were written altogether?

Curriculum links

Most children have had some contact with chain letters and are fascinated by them. Indeed, some adults cannot resist the promises of chain letters even though experience has shown that they rarely fulfil these promises. This activity shows how a chain letter system works. It provides opportunities for the children to look for patterns and in so doing develop multiplication skills.

DISCUSSING AND SOLVING THE PROBLEM

The ideal time to present this activity is when a child brings along a chain letter they have received or talks about a chain letter someone else received. However, if this does not happen, invent a situation of your own to tell the children about. Allow time for the class to talk about chain letters they have been involved with. Then present the problem. Let the children read it silently, then choose one or two children to read it aloud. Ask some children to explain what they have to work out, emphasising that they must work out how many letters were written altogether, not just the number at each stage.

Put the children in groups and ask them to decide how they are going to try to work this out. However, don't let them start working it out yet. After a few minutes, ask the spokesperson for each group to tell the other groups how they are going to work it out. We found most groups wanted to draw a diagram. One group wanted to act it out by cutting up paper to represent letters. This group was tempted to change their strategy after hearing the other groups, but we encouraged them to follow this through.

Now set the groups to work. You will find it interesting to see how they do their diagrams. Most groups start and then realise they have not spread out the diagram enough and as a result it is cramped up in the top right-hand corner. Let them do it again if they wish. While we were waiting for the group who was cutting up paper to finish, we set the other groups the task of exploring how many letters would be written if Alice had written to six friends who each wrote to six friends etc.

When the groups have finished, let them share their work to show 155 letters written altogether. Discuss the strategies groups used and decide if each method was equally effective. Encourage the children to look for the pattern in the numbers, i.e. $1 \times 5 = 5$, $5 \times 5 = 25$, $25 \times 5 = 125$ etc.

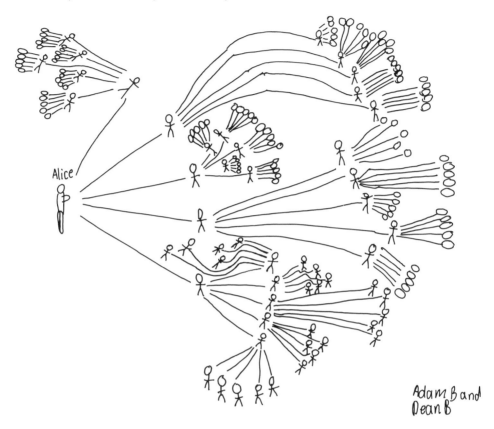

Adam B and
Dean B

BUILDING ON THE ACTIVITY

❑ Explore how many letters would be written if Alice had written to six friends. If some groups have already started this, ask them to describe how they are going about working it out. They should be able to use the pattern from the previous activity to work this out. Encourage them to do so. Can they use this pattern to work out other numbers of chain letters?

> *This is an excellent pattern-and-order activity in its own right, and the experiences of drawing expanding diagrams and cutting up bits of paper will be a valuable basis to the children at a later stage when they are introduced to exponential notation.*

26 | Sheep pens

At shearing time the farmer needed to separate his sheep into lambs, ewes, rams, shorn, unshorn, injured etc. He had a large square holding pen with posts set out like this:

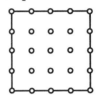

He had sections of fencing that fitted between the posts so that he could close off smaller areas of the big pen. How many different square pens could he make?

Curriculum links

The children set out to explore a problem about space and shape and in fact end up making discoveries about sets of number patterns.

DISCUSSING AND SOLVING THE PROBLEM

After the children have read the problem silently and aloud, choose a child to explain what they have to find out and to demonstrate on the chalkboard how fences can be placed from post to post to create new pens. Give each child a copy of page 103 and a supply of used matchsticks to represent the sections of fencing.

Put them in groups and set them to work. The children of course have no difficulty in using the matches to make pens; they find it more difficult to keep track of the number of different pens they have made. Move about the room and watch as the groups work out a methodical way to count the different pens they make. They are quick to find the 16 small pens (one matchstick per side) and at least four of the 2-matchstick-per-side pens. Then they notice that the larger pens can overlap and many will start to lose track of their counting at this stage.

This is a good moment to stop for a share time and to listen to what the groups have discovered so far. Ask particularly if any of the groups has worked out a way of keeping a tally of the different pens being made and encourage all groups to keep some sort of orderly record. For instance:

pens with 1 matchstick-long fences	16
pens with 2 matchstick-long fences	9 ⎫ Add
pens with 3 matchstick-long fences	4 ⎬ these
pens with 4 matchstick-long fences	1 ⎭ later

Let the groups continue working until at least some of them have found all 30 pens.

Have another share time for groups to tell about their work and the total number of pens they made. Let them help you fill in the numbers missing from the above table. Discuss the table with the children and see what number patterns they recognise in it.

BUILDING ON THE ACTIVITY

❑ Ask the children how many pens could be made if the large pen were only three matchsticks per side instead of four. They can alter their sheet accordingly and use the matchsticks to help them work this out, or some may be able to arrive at an answer by extrapolating from the number pattern in the table above. When the children have an answer, let them help you add another column of figures to the table:

size of large pen	3 sticks	4 sticks
pens with 1 matchstick-long fences	9	16
pens with 2 matchstick-long fences	4	9
pens with 3 matchstick-long fences	1	4
pens with 4 matchstick-long fences	0	1

The children may now be ready to predict answers for large pens that have sides two matchsticks long, one matchstick long and five matchsticks long.

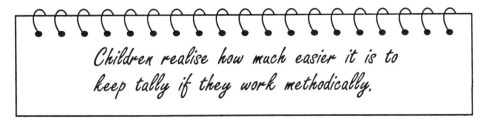

Children realise how much easier it is to keep tally if they work methodically.

27

Making posters

You have a piece of A4 paper which is 21 cm high and about 30 cm wide to make a poster to advertise your school fête (or other current event). You need to leave a border of 3 cm all the way around your poster. (You can rule this in pencil so that it can be erased later.) You will need four lines of writing to tell people WHAT (school fête), WHEN (the date), TIME (morning, afternoon etc.), WHERE (school address). You should make each line of writing the same height and leave equal spaces between each line of writing. How high will you make the writing on your poster?

Curriculum links

We decided to do this after watching children struggle with poster layout. Many children start a poster and find they run out of space, so that the information at the bottom of the poster is squashed into a tiny area. Others use trial and error to rule lines for writing and find that they need so many goes at doing this that their page looks a mess before they start. This activity provides excellent measuring practice for children, as well as giving them an appreciation of design.

DISCUSSING AND SOLVING THE PROBLEM

After you have made sure that the children understand what they are asked to do, give each group a sheet of A4 paper and let them start work. Almost every one of our groups ruled their border in pencil and then reverted to trial-and-error to try to fit in four evenly spaced lines for writing.

At this point it is a good idea to call the groups together and discuss how else to approach the problem. Some suggestions were:

- decide on a height for the letters, e.g. 2 cm or 3 cm and then work out how much room will be left for spaces between the lines;

- divide the page in half horizontally and then in half again so that each of these sections will contain a line of writing and a space;

- divide the remaining 15 cm by 4, which means the letters must be no more than 3 cm high and there will be a total of 3 cm left for spaces between lines.

Let the children go back to work and discuss with the others in their group how to use any of these suggestions to come up with a format. When the groups have completed their poster, display them and let each group tell how they worked out their poster layout.

BUILDING ON THE ACTIVITY

❑ Have the children collect commercial posters, invitations, greeting cards, display advertisements from newspapers, etc. They should use rulers to measure the height of the letters and the spaces between lines of writing. Can the children see any conventions that designers use for the layout of this kind of material?

The amount of real measuring that the children do in this activity is invaluable.

28

Lunch-time

George bought a plain hamburger and a chocolate milkshake for lunch and paid $1.50. Ahmed bought two plain hamburgers and a strawberry milkshake and the cashier charged him $2.40. When the two boys compared the price of their lunches, Ahmed thought he had been charged too much. What do you think?

Curriculum links

The children will have to solve this money problem by trial and error. Their main hurdle is to adopt a methodical approach rather than relying on random guesswork.

DISCUSSING AND SOLVING THE PROBLEM

After the children have read the problem, you will find that some need help to specify exactly what they have to find out. Some will be content to say things like, 'That sounds like the right price', and other will say 'He paid too much.'. It is not until you ask these children to justify their answers that they realise they must work out the exact price of a milkshake and the exact price of a hamburger.

Once all the children accept that they need to do this, then put them in groups and let them get started. Some children may have difficulty working out how to begin. If they have still not made any progress after a few minutes, stop the class for a share time and let other groups explain how they started by guessing the price of either the hamburgers or the milkshakes. Use this opportunity to encourage the children to write down how they are working out the problem. Move about the room and see which groups are using the information from their first guess to make a more accurate second guess, and which groups are making random guesses.

When the groups have found that the hamburgers cost 90c and the milkshakes cost 60c, give each group the opportunity to report to the class how they worked it out. Choose the groups who used a totally random method to go first and invite the others to comment on how their guesses could have been more efficient.

Some will have managed to produce a table similar to this:

Cost of hamburgers		Cost of milkshakes	Cost of Ahmed's lunch
Guess 1	70c	$1.50—70c = 80c	70c + 70c + 80c = $2.20 *too low*
Guess 2	75c	$1.50—75c = 75c	75c + 75c + 75c = $2.25 *too low*
Guess 3	80c	$1.50—80c = 70c	80c + 80c + 70c = $2.30 *too low*
Guess 4	90c	$1.50—90c = 60c	90c + 90c + 60c = $2.40 *correct*

BUILDING ON THE ACTIVITY

❑ Once the children see that this problem is based on very simple arithmetic, they enjoy making up similar problems of their own for other children to solve. It works well if all the children stick to the same theme (e.g. lunches, clothes, CD's and records etc.) and their questions are collected in book form. You can choose a theme, such as cars or electrical goods, if you want to provide practice in working with larger numbers.

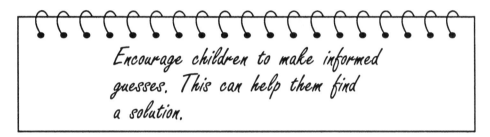

Encourage children to make informed guesses. This can help them find a solution.

29 Good news travels fast

When a baby girl was born at 6 a.m. her parents phoned one person immediately to tell them the good news. This person phoned two others within 5 minutes. So by 6.05 a.m. apart from the parents, three people knew. The second two each phoned two others within 5 minutes. This continued until 6.30 a.m. How many people had heard the good news by then?

Curriculum links

This activity is similar to 'Letter writing' (activity 25) but has a time component added to make it more challenging. Most children find it difficult to picture that so many people would hear the news in only 30 minutes. It provides opportunities for the children to look for patterns in doubling and to practise counting by twos. We recommend you do the 'Letter writing' activity some time before you do this activity.

DISCUSSING AND SOLVING THE PROBLEM

Most children will need to read this problem two or three times and talk about it before they are sure of what it means. The time factor in it seems to confuse them temporarily. If they have already done 'Letter writing' they may comment on the similarities. If they do, ask them to talk about it, focusing on the strategies they used to work it out. If no-one recognises the similarities, draw their attention to it and then focus on the strategies they used. Ask the children if they think they will be able to use the same strategies for this problem, i.e. drawing a diagram, acting it out and so on. You will probably find most children think you can, but a few are still confused by the time element. This is a good time to have them think about how they are going to deal with this.

Put the children in groups and ask them to decide how they are going to try to work this out. Don't let them start working it out yet. After a short time, ask a representative from each group to tell the other groups what they have decided. We found our groups either wanted to

- draw a diagram which branched out like a tree and include the five-minute intervals above each set of 'branches', or
- draw a chart which showed each five minutes and use counters to represent the people.

72

Before we set the groups to work we asked some children to guess how many people they thought would hear the good news in the 30 minutes. We didn't give them time to think very hard about this. Their guesses ranged from 30 to 100, with most being nearer 30.

Once the children start work, move around watching what they do. We found our groups coped very well. They remembered a lot about drawing diagrams from the 'Letter writing' activity and also that they had to add the number of people at each stage together to find the total of people who knew about the birth. They found the time element was easier to handle than they had thought.

When your groups have finished, let them share their work to show that 127 people would know about the birth. Discuss the strategies the groups used and decide if any method was more effective than the others. Encourage children to look for the pattern in the numbers, i.e. $1 \times 2 = 2$, $2 \times 2 = 4$, $4 \times 2 = 8$, $8 \times 2 = 16$, $16 \times 2 = 32$ etc. Finish by comparing the answer with the guesses children made at the start.

BUILDING ON THE ACTIVITY

❑ Use calculators and the pattern found above to work out how many people would know about the birth after one hour if the calls continued in the same manner.

❑ Calculate the cost of making this many phone calls assuming they were all local calls. This could lead to a discussion about whether this is a good method of passing on news. Our children agreed that it certainly shared the cost and was a quick way of spreading news, but that sometimes it was nicer to talk to people yourself.

Try to display some of the diagrams completed by the groups. Too often mathematics is the only subject that is not displayed.

30 Bells

The city councillors installed a bell on the Town Hall clock so that it chimed on the hour. They were pleased that it sounded so impressive. But soon the people living nearby were complaining. 'Do you know how many times a day I have to listen to that bell?' complained one lady. Can you work out how many times a day the bell chimed?

Curriculum links

Children are usually most impressed when they work out the total number of times the bell chimes each day. This example of adding consecutive numbers can be solved in a number of ways by the children. With some assistance they can also discover some neat numerical shortcuts and some interesting number patterns.

When we did this activity we also found some children had stories about noisy bells that they wanted to share with the class.

DISCUSSING AND SOLVING THE PROBLEM

After the children have read the question, ask them to predict how many times they think the bell will chime in one day. The answers usually range from 12 to 60. Write these guesses on the chalkboard. Ask the class why the answer could not be as low as 12—make sure they all understand that the bell will chime to indicate what hour it is, that is once for one o'clock, twice for two o'clock, three times for three o'clock . . . up to twelve times for twelve o'clock. Make sure they also remember that there are 24 hours in a complete day, not just 12. Once they all have this information, ask the groups to discuss how they will go about finding the total number of chimes in a day. After a minute or so, ask a member from each group to report back to the whole class what method their group will be using. The most common response is to add up the numbers from 1 to 12 and then double the answer.

Give the groups time to do this and stop for another share time when most groups have found the answer of 156. Have the children compare this answer with their initial guesses written on the board. Now ask one group member to show on the board how their group actually worked out the answer.

They will probably write something like this:

+ 1
+ 2
+ 3 (6)
+ 4 (10)
+ 5 (15)
+ 6 (21)
+ 7 (28)
+ 8 (36)
+ 9 (45)
+ 10 (55)
+ 11 (66)
+ 12 (78)   × 2 = 156 chimes per day.

Ask the children if they can see a shorter way of adding up the numbers 1 to 12. Show them how the numbers can be paired to make a set of six 12's:

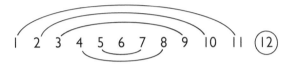

with the number 6 left unpaired.

So a quicker way to add the numbers would be:
$$6 \times 12 = 72 \ + 6 = 78$$

BUILDING ON THE ACTIVITY

❑ Ask the children to use this method to add up how many dots there are on a dice ($3 \times 6 = 18 \ + 3 = 21$). Ask some children to demonstrate their working out on the chalkboard.

❑ Challenge the children to add up the numbers 1 to 100 (5050), and then 1 to 1000 (500 500).

Children are most impressed with the way in which this shortcut gives them the power to deal with large numbers so easily.

31 Rescue attempt

When the floodwaters came, Daniel and Tim were left stranded on the roof of their house with their father and uncle. Their uncle had managed to grab the inflatable dinghy, but it was only a small one and could carry no more than one adult or two children at a time. Could they use the dinghy to get all of them across the water to the roadway before the floodwaters rose any higher?

Curriculum links

Many children find this problem a real challenge. Even after they decide on a strategy they cannot think enough steps ahead to feel confident of finding an answer. For many it is a test of faith that the step-by-step application of logic will eventually lead to a solution.

DISCUSSING AND SOLVING THE PROBLEM

After they have read the problem, most children can confidently explain what they are being asked to find out. If you put them straight into their working groups and ask them to decide on a strategy for solving the problem, most groups will be quick to decide that acting out the situation is the best method: either by each person in the group 'becoming' one of the characters in the story and moving across and back a designated stretch of water, or by using objects to represent the people and moving them back and forth across a table or similar space. Some groups decide that they can find an answer by drawing diagrams on paper and some groups think they will reach an answer by just talking it through step by step. Ask one person from each group to tell the class what method their group will be using. Some groups do change their strategy at this stage.

Now ask the children to try out their method to see what answer they come up with. Suggest that they choose someone in their group to write down each step of the process. Some groups manage to work straight through to a solution. Many others get stuck after the first crossing because they do not realise that, after crossing over to the roadway, people can be returned to the rooftop to help rescue the others. If several groups are stuck at this point, it is worthwhile to stop for a share time so that the more successful groups can describe how they overcame this difficulty. This is usually enough assistance for most groups to be able to continue step by step to get all the people across the water. You will hear the excited pitch in the children's voices as they realise they have solved the problem!

This is often followed about half a minute later by a tone of despair when they realise that nobody in the group wrote down what was happening and that nobody can remember exactly what they did. So they need to start all over again and usually have their solution recorded within a few minutes.

At share time let each group demonstrate how they found their answer. The groups who chose pen-and-paper methods may want to draw their solution on the chalkboard. It will probably look something like this:

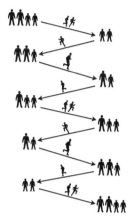

- The two boys cross to the roadway, then one returns to the roof.
- One of the adults crosses over and the other child returns to the roof.
- Both boys cross over again and only one returns.
- The other adult then crosses to the roadway and the other boy comes back to the roof to collect his brother.
- They both return to the roadway.

BUILDING ON THE ACTIVITY

❑ Having solved this problem, or even just seeing how other children worked it out, gets most children enthusiastic about working on similar problems. There are many variations on this problem, for example:

A little boy is taking his pets to school for pet day. He has his rabbit on a leash, he is carrying a bag of vegetables for the rabbit's lunch, and his dog Toby is following behind. When he comes to the school-crossing he has a problem: he can't trust Toby to cross the road alone and he is only strong enough to carry the vegetables, the rabbit or the dog one at a time across the road. Toby will bite the rabbit if he is not there and the rabbit will eat the vegetables if they are left together. How can he get everything across the road safely? (Carry the rabbit over and tie him up, go back and carry the vegetables over and the rabbit back, tie up the rabbit and carry the dog over, then go back for the rabbit!)

Having solved two or three of these problems, some children will feel confident to make up their own version for other children to solve.

This activity is a great confidence booster for the children who lack belief in their ability to think things through logically.

32 Water jugs

We need to measure out five cups of water. We do not have a cup. All we have are two jugs, one which we know holds exactly seven cups and the other which we know holds exactly three cups. How can we use these two jugs to measure out five cups of water?

Curriculum links

At first some children will say this cannot be done or they will try to explain how it can be done using other jugs, bowls etc. Make sure all the children understand that the task can be done and that no other equipment is necessary. It is a good idea to have some jugs and a cup available for each group so that groups can work out and place markings at the 3-cup and 7-cup levels on each of their jugs before they begin the task. You will also need some buckets of water available for filling and emptying the jugs. The links with volume are obvious.

DISCUSSING AND SOLVING THE PROBLEM

When you are discussing this with the children, make sure they all understand that when working out this problem no other containers apart from the two jugs and the supply of water are needed. When the children are explaining the problem to you in their own words, it will be obvious to you whether they understand it or not.

After ascertaining that all our children understood what the task was, we asked each group to decide what it needed to help solve the problem. After each group had time to discuss this, we brought the groups back to the floor to share their information with everyone. Most groups chose to use containers (at this stage we had these out of sight), but a couple of groups said they thought they could work with drawings to represent the two jugs. This share time again gives the teacher a chance to check that all groups understand the problem.

We showed the containers to the children and asked them how they could make these hold 3 and 7 cups. After some discussion it was decided to use a cup to fill each container and mark with a waterproof pen the level where 3 cups came to on one and where 7 cups came to on the other. The groups who had decided to use containers set to work, returning their cup when they were finished. All groups worked hard at finding a solution but began to get frustrated at their lack of success, so we called them all together again.

We asked some groups to tell what they had tried. The two groups who were drawing pictures showed what they had been doing and it was obvious from the drawings that they could measure 4 cups. We discussed this and found that all the groups had got to this stage, i.e. they had filled the 7-cup jug and poured from it into the 3-cup jug, leaving 4 cups in the 7-cup jug. So we provided them with a clue for the next stage: 'You need to have 1 cup of water in the 3-cup jug', and let them start work again. It wasn't long before we heard cries of joy from one corner! We quickly asked them to check their solution and if it was correct, to write it down. We also asked them not to tell other groups. Very soon other shrieks followed and the few remaining groups who had not managed to work it out, demanded to know how to do it.

Rather than make them all complete the task, we allowed the groups to share the solution now:

- After the first stage they had emptied the 3-cup jug and then filled it again from the 4 cups left in their 7-cup jug.
- This had left 1 cup in the 7-cup jug, and the 3-cup jug full.
- They emptied the 3-cup jug and poured the 1 cup into it.
- They then filled the 7-cup jug and poured into the 3-cup jug until it was full.
- Because it already had 1 cup in it, it took 2 more cups to fill it, thereby leaving 5 cups in the 7-cup jug.

BUILDING ON THE ACTIVITY

❑ Ask each group, especially those who used the equipment, to draw a pictorial representation of this task showing each stage clearly.

❑ Work out what other amounts you can measure using only these two jugs.

As soon as a few groups have succeeded in working out the problem, the other groups cannot contain their curiosity. It is unfair to make them continue, unless they really want to.

33 Wages

James was offered a job splitting wood at the local wood-yard. He had to decide how he was going to be paid. His boss gave him a choice of either

- $100 per week, or
- each week he gets $1 the first day, $2 the second day, $4 the third day, $8 the fourth day and so on, doubling the money each day up to seven days.

Which would you take?

Curriculum links

Most children will immediately opt for the $100. It seems like a fortune to them and they start working out how they will spend it. Few stop to think whether the lowly amounts mentioned in the second option will actually add up to any large amount. By working through the second option the children will realise the power of doubling. This can lead to further investigations in doubling and halving.

DISCUSSING AND SOLVING THE PROBLEM

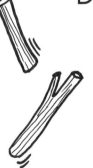

We suggest that you give the children only a brief time to read the question and make their initial choice. We have found that most children will gladly accept the $100 and not bother to check further. Tell the children that if you were James you would choose the second method of payment, and watch their reaction. It generally ranges from scoffs at a silly suggestion to children racing for a calculator or pen and paper to work out just how much the second option will pay.

Suggest that all groups work out how much money the second method of payment will total. Let them decide how to work this out. Groups we have seen have used mental arithmetic, various pen-and-paper methods, calculators and toy money. When the children have worked out that the second option would pay $127, many still show disbelief and need to see that other groups using different methods all reached the same answer as they did. A share time is invaluable for this.

BUILDING ON THE ACTIVITY

❑ To demonstrate to the children what a dramatic effect doubling can have, ask them what would have happened if James had worked only a 5-day or a 6-day week. They will see that working just one day less, it would be better for James to take the first option.

❑ Let the children work out how much money James would get if his boss continued to double his pay each day for another seven days!

❑ Tell the groups to act as bosses to work out a scale of pay that uses doubling for their employees. Give them some guidelines, for example start at $3 for the first day, continue doubling for a 5- or 7-day week, then work out a lump sum alternative payment to offer. The groups could present these to the class, who could then work out the better option in each case.

Toy money and calculators are invaluable for getting the most out of this activity.

We always send something to Grandma on her birthday. This year we sent a CD. The lady at our local post office said the package would cost $3.10 to send. When she checked her stamp books she found she only had four $1.50-stamps, eight 70-cent stamps and twenty 40-cent stamps. She couldn't work out how we could put the correct postage on the package. Can you?

Curriculum links

Most children start to solve this problem by using trial and error. Many soon notice that certain combinations are not possible and begin to explore patterns or sequences of stamps in search of their answer. This question provides valuable practice in adding money amounts mentally and also in creating number patterns.

DISCUSSING AND SOLVING THE PROBLEM

Some children will be unfamiliar with having to use different stamps to make up a set amount of postage; they will only have had to put single stamps on standard letters. After a short discussion about how postage rates change according to the weight of the package and the distance the package is being sent, these children will be confident that they understand the basic problem.

Put the children in groups and give each group a copy of page 104 to work with. Ask them to start by deciding how they will go about finding a solution. Most of our groups reported back that they decided to cut out the stamps and try them in different arrangements until they found a group that added up to $3.10. After about five minutes none of the groups had found a solution, but some had worked out that you could only use one of the $1.50-stamps (because two $1.50-stamps came to $3.00 and there were no 10c-stamps to make up the amount to $3.10). Therefore they were looking for combinations of 40c- and 70c-stamps that totalled $1.60 to put with the $1.50-stamp to make $3.10 altogether. Once they explained this to the other groups, everyone set to work with renewed enthusiasm and most groups had an answer very shortly afterwards ($1.50, 40c, 40c, 40c, 40c).

At this point we had a short share time and let one member from each group report on their group's findings. Then we let the children know that there are actually two solutions to the problem and asked them to continue working to find the second solution. Some groups went back to randomly shuffling stamps into different combinations, but several other groups used the information they had already established to narrow down the problem. They remembered that it is only possible to use one $1.50-stamp and this had been done in the first solution, so their other solution did not contain any $1.50-stamps, only 40c- and 70c-stamps. We let them share this information with the other groups and it was not long before everyone had found the second solution (six 40c-stamps and one 70c-stamp).

At share time it was interesting to note that some groups had continued to work by trial and error using the 40c- and 70c-stamps, and that others had used reasoning in an attempt to be more methodical. One group even recorded their working out like this:

8 × 40c = $3.20	*too much*
7 × 40c = $2.80	*leaves 30c, 40c + 30c = 70c, so*
6 × 40c = $2.40	*plus 70c = $3.10*

BUILDING ON THE ACTIVITY

❑ Ask your school secretary to bring in the morning's mail and let the children see the different forms of postage that are possible: stamps, pre-paid mail, franked mail etc.

❑ Are there different amounts of postage on the letters that have stamps on them? What denomination of stamps have been used? Which is the most valuable letter in the batch? Why do you think this is—because it is the biggest envelope? the heaviest? has travelled the greatest distance?

Stamps seem to have an instant attraction.
Children kept bringing stamps to school and
soon we had collected enough to make a poster.

Mystery story

Marta has been reading a mystery story and when the doorbell rings she leaves the book open on the coffee table. While she is at the door her nephew decides to close her book. When Marta returns to her book she is annoyed to find that she does not know which page she was up to. Her nephew says, 'I can see you like mysteries, so let's see if you can solve this one. When I closed your book I noticed that the product of the facing pages was 7140.' Can you help Marta solve her mystery?

Curriculum links

This is not a difficult problem for most children but it is interesting to watch how they go about solving it. Once they understand the task, the methods they choose to work it out will tell you a lot about their estimation and number sense. It is a good idea to have calculators available for this activity.

DISCUSSING AND SOLVING THE PROBLEM

There are a lot of words in this problem. Most of them are there purely to tell the story but can confuse children if they don't really understand what they have to do. When you are discussing what the problem actually is, it helps to show the children an open book and point out the facing pages. Let some children act out the story and choose pages to leave the book open at. We used a book with only ten pages so that we could focus on what 'product' meant. Our first child left the book open at pages 4 and 5. We closed the book and told the others that the product was 20. They realised very quickly that the pages had to have been 4 and 5. We repeated this a few times. In this particular case the strategy of using smaller numbers is effective as a demonstration of the meaning of 'product'.

Once all the children knew what they had to do, the groups set off to solve the mystery. You will probably find that most groups use trial and error. Here it is interesting to note which groups just pick numbers 'out of the air' and which base their choice on a known fact. For example, one of our groups said that the numbers would have to be larger than 50 because 50×50 is 2500. Another of our groups knew this fact and also that $60 \times 60 = 3600$, $70 \times 70 = 4900$, $80 \times 80 = 6400$ and $90 \times 90 = 8100$. Therefore they estimated correctly that the two numbers they were looking for were between 80 and 90. When they had narrowed their choices down this far, this group began looking for the two consecutive numbers whose final digits would give 0 when multiplied together. This left them with 80 and 81, 84 and 85, 85 and 86, and 89 and 90. It did not take long from here to work out that the two numbers they wanted were 84 and 85.

Other groups found the same answer in less systematic ways, but all used some estimation and practised the mechanics of multiplication. Our share time at the end focused on the way each group went about solving the mystery. All were impressed with the way described above.

$$
\begin{array}{r}
\overset{7}{7}8 \\
\times\ \overset{5}{7}9 \\
\hline
702 \\
5460 \\
\hline
7862 \\
6162
\end{array}
\qquad
\begin{array}{r}
7\overset{4}{7} \\
\times\overset{4}{7}8 \\
\hline
616 \\
5390 \\
\hline
6006
\end{array}
\qquad
\begin{array}{r}
\overset{4}{6}7 \\
\times\ 68 \\
\hline
536 \\
4020 \\
\hline
4556
\end{array}
\qquad
\begin{array}{r}
\overset{5}{8}7 \\
\times88 \\
\hline
696 \\
6960 \\
\hline
8046 \\
7656
\end{array}
\qquad
\begin{array}{r}
\overset{4}{7}\overset{6}{6} \\
\times\ 77 \\
\hline
532 \\
5320 \\
\hline
5852
\end{array}
\qquad
\begin{array}{r}
81 \\
\times82 \\
\hline
162 \\
6480 \\
\hline
6642
\end{array}
$$

$$
\begin{array}{r}
\overset{1}{8}3 \\
\times\ 84 \\
\hline
332 \\
6640 \\
\hline
6972
\end{array}
\qquad
\begin{array}{r}
\overset{4}{8}5 \\
\times\ 86 \\
\hline
510 \\
6800 \\
\hline
7310
\end{array}
\begin{array}{r}
\overset{3}{8}4 \\
\times85 \\
\hline
420 \\
6720 \\
\hline
7140
\end{array}
$$

BUILDING ON THE ACTIVITY

❑ During the share time we discovered quite a lot of children who seemed to be realising for the first time that number facts such as 50×50 and 60×60 were the same pattern as for the tables, and that if you knew this pattern you could use it to help solve other number facts. We decided to list these number facts on the chalkboard with the answers, e.g.

$10 \times 10 = 100$
$20 \times 20 = 400$
$30 \times 30 = 900$
$40 \times 40 = 1600$ etc.

The children looked for other patterns and were intrigued by the amount with which each answer increased.

❑ We now presented groups with another book mystery to solve. This time all the groups used the known number facts to help them find the two consecutive numbers.

Sometimes children just need to be shown the links between number facts to enable them to work more effectively.

36 | Parking lot

The company directors had bought a vacant block of land 30 m × 50 m in the centre of the city so they could build a new office tower. While they were waiting for the building permits to be approved they decided to raise some money by using the land as a parking lot. If they allowed an area 3 m × 6 m for each car, how many car spaces could they fit on their parking lot?

Curriculum links

Many children can recall temporary parking lots set up on vacant building sites and have actually been with a parent trying to manoeuvre the family car into a tiny parking space. Even though most children end up solving this problem in a very concrete way, it provides them with useful experience of scale and ratio, shape, pattern, area, measurement and addition.

DISCUSSING AND SOLVING THE PROBLEM

Choose several children to explain the situation outlined in the problem, what information is provided and what they are being asked to find out. Most children can picture the situation clearly enough but are not sure how they can actually work out a solution.

Put the children into groups and ask them to discuss how they could find out how many car spaces can be fitted into an area this size. Most children intuitively know that first of all they need to make a model or plan of the site, but when they sketch an oblong and label the sides 30 m and 50 m, they don't find this much of a help. This is a good point to stop so the groups can share their ideas.

Usually you will find at least one group who wants to make a scale drawing of the lot, using a scale of 1 cm = 1 m. You can make it easier for them by providing sheets of plain paper large enough for them to draw a 30 cm × 50 cm rectangle. Now ask the groups to discuss how they will proceed from here and give them a few minutes to talk about it. When they report back, you will find some groups who planned to rule 3 cm × 6 cm rectangles directly on to their sheet and other groups who decided to cut out a stack of 3 cm × 6 cm cards so they could try various arrangements of these to see which one accommodates the most cars. It only takes a short discussion for children to see that the second strategy will probably save them a lot of time (and rubbing out) in the long run.

From here it is best to let the children continue without interruption until they have reached their solution. As you move about the groups, you will hear much discussion about the room needed to manoeuvre cars in and out of parking spaces and you will see the children doing test-runs around their parking lot using small cards as cars. You may need to discuss this with groups who have forgotten to leave space for cars to get in and out—as a guide, they should leave at least one car-length (6 m) for the cars to be able to get in and out of a car space. The children will also realise that they must have an entrance and exit for the cars somewhere on the plan. Let them place these wherever is most suitable for their design.

When the children are satisfied with their solution, let them paste the small cards into position. Most children then want to add more detail to make their lot more realistic—outlining each space, entry and exit gates (some want to make boom gates), cashier's booth etc. When the children have finished their parking lot, let them display it for the class to see and explain how and why they decided on their final arrangement. Groups who fit more than 40 car spaces into their lot have used their space efficiently.

BUILDING ON THE ACTIVITY

❑ Discuss the difference in parking arrangements between used car-yards and parking lots. Why is this so? How many cars could you fit on the 30 m × 50 m site if it was being used as a car-yard?

❑ Some children are surprised that a car needs so much space. Work out how many car spaces would fit in your classroom. **Working strictly under adult supervision**, have the children check the dimensions of a car in the school car-park. How much extra room do they need to allow so that doors can be opened?

❑ This activity can be combined with activity 14, 'Parking fees', so children can work out how much money it is possible to raise from their parking lot in one day.

Choosing the right moment to interrupt the class so they can share their ideas can result in children being rescued from frustration and failure and given the chance to experience success.

37 | **Pocket money**

My brother Jack earns extra money by collecting aluminium cans. He hates squashing them flat, so he lets me do that and he pays me $2 for each large bag of squashed cans. Last Saturday morning I had been squashing cans for an hour when my friend Alex came over and asked if he could help. I said, 'O.K.' but he was really slow and only did half the cans that I did. It took another hour to finish the job with both of us working. I thought it was only fair to pay Alex for the work that he did, but I couldn't work out how much I should pay him. Can you?

Curriculum links

Children relate well to this problem—it is sometimes hard to interrupt the discussion about pocket money to get on with solving the problem. Working out their solution provides the children with useful practice at dealing with fractions and money.

DISCUSSING AND SOLVING THE PROBLEM

Having read the problem through, the children can explain the situation clearly and know that they have to find out how much to pay Alex. They are not sure how the information provided can be used to work this out.

Put the children in groups and tell them to write down all the information the problem tells them and to talk about how they can use these facts to work out an answer. Try to give the children just long enough to decide their strategy without going on to work out their answer. Choose a person from each group to tell the class what method their group has decided on. Many groups decide to draw a diagram (but are not really sure what it is going to look like until they have finished it); others get cubes or counters to represent cans and try to work it out that way. Few children at this stage realise that getting an answer will depend on using fractions.

Set the children back to work and move about the room to see and hear how they apply their method. The greatest difficulty they have to overcome is that they don't know how many cans were crushed in the first hour, so they don't have any numbers to work with. They intuitively have to find a way to represent this unknown number so they can work out the rest of the problem. Some end up representing this number with area: they draw a diagram showing the number of cans crushed in the first hour as a bag or a pile of a particular size:

cans crushed in the first hour   **cans crushed in the second hour**

by Jack's brother   by Jack's brother   by Alex

The groups using counters find themselves nominating a number for the cans crushed in the first hour and putting out a stack of counters to show this. If they choose a 'round' number like 100 they reach the solution more easily than if they choose, say, 57.

Once they have completed their models, the children can see that Jack's brother crushed four times as many cans as Alex or that Alex crushed $\frac{1}{5}$ as many cans as Jack's brother. So, they argue, Alex should get $\frac{1}{5}$ of the $2, or 40 cents. At share time, make sure both these methods are demonstrated.

You may also find a group that uses a different method, reasoning that it would have taken Jack's brother another half-hour to finish the cans without Alex. So if he was paid $2 for $2\frac{1}{2}$ hours' work, this is 40 cents per half-hour. Since Alex really only did $\frac{1}{2}$ hour's work, he should be paid 40 cents.

BUILDING ON THE ACTIVITY

❑ Investigating children's pocket money provides a wealth of mathematical ideas. You can find out about how much on average children get, how this varies with age, whether it is earnt or given, what jobs children do to earn their money, how long these take and, of course, how the money is spent. You can also investigate ways for children to earn money that don't rely on parents' generosity, such as paper rounds, collecting cans and so on.

Encourage the children to draw a picture or make a model of a problem — it will often lead them straight to an answer.

38

Roll out the red carpet

We are going to make a 'carpet' out of sheets of red paper (50 cm × 30 cm) as shown in the diagram. So that the 'carpet' stays together we will use tape to join each piece of paper and to stick the paper to the floor. How much tape will we need to make a 'carpet' 30 metres long?

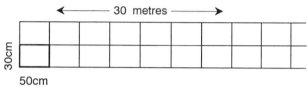

← 30 metres →

30cm

50cm

Curriculum links

This activity came about as a result of the children wanting to make a special visitor feel welcome. Apart from a morning tea, the children wanted to give the visitor the 'red carpet' treatment and decided that if they taped red paper down the length of the corridor where their visitor entered the building, it would create the desired effect! Before they could do this however they had to check that they had enough tape and paper. This activity has many links with area and perimeter.

DISCUSSING AND SOLVING THE PROBLEM

You need to create a similar situation to that mentioned above. If there is no-one visiting, perhaps a story or film could lead into this. Once the children have decided on the 'red carpet' treatment, their first step is to measure the length of the area where the carpet is to go. Have children work in groups to do this and then give each group one piece of the paper that will be used. (It does not matter if the paper you use is a different size to that used in the diagram. The length of your 'carpet' will probably vary too.)

Let the groups decide how to calculate how much paper they will need from this one piece.

- We found a couple of groups who said they couldn't do it unless they had more paper, as they needed to actually put it down the corridor!
- Other groups used their one piece of paper as a measurer along the corridor and either counted by twos as they went or doubled the amount at the end.
- One or two groups used pen and paper and calculators to come up with an answer.

When all the groups have arrived at an answer, let them share the methods they used. With this stage completed, the next step is to work out how much tape will be needed to lay the 'carpet'. Use some of the paper to start a 'carpet' and point out where the tape will go, i.e. to join each piece together fully on each side, as well as around the outside of the 'carpet' to stick it to the floor. In groups, ask the children to suggest how they could work this out. We found that all the groups drew a diagram and came up with a variety of methods for doing it. Some suggestions for our 30 metres of 'carpet' were:

- to multiply the length by 3 (90 metres) and add to this 60 cm for every row, and an extra 60 cm for the end (36 metres and 60 cm), which makes a total of 126 metres and 60 cm of tape;
- to work out how much tape is needed for every two pieces of paper and keep adding until we reach 60 pieces (or multiply by 60), and then add one more 60 cm for the end (210 cm × 60 + 60 cm);
- to keep adding 60 cm and 150 cm until we reach the end of our carpet.

BUILDING ON THE ACTIVITY

❑ Ask the children what they could do so that they would use less tape but still have a 'carpet' the same length and width. Some suggestions:

- If each piece of paper was longer, less tape would be needed;
- Use wider paper so that you only needed one sheet width;
- Use less tape by not putting it all the way around the edges.

❑ Ask groups to investigate what would happen if they turned the sheets of paper around the other way so that the 'carpet' was 1 metre wide and each section was 30 cm long. Would they need more, less or the same number of pieces of paper? How much tape would be needed for this 'carpet'?

There are many effective strategies that the children can use to solve this problem.

39

Knock-out

Thirty-two players compete in a 'knock-out' tennis tournament. Each player plays a first-round match against one other player and the winner goes into the second round. The loser drops out. This continues until there are only two players left. They play a final to decide the champion. Tournament organisers need to know how many matches will be played so they can schedule matches and sell tickets. Can you work out how many matches are played altogether?

Curriculum links

We have found that many children are not familiar with tournaments of this type. Most sporting events they take part in are 'round robins'. Therefore, it is important to spend time discussing sports that do have knock-out tournaments, such as tennis and squash, and that once a player is beaten, they are out of the tournament. Let the children talk about competitive sports they are involved in. For this activity the children will need to use their knowledge of number patterns to find an answer and work out how to represent their information visually.

DISCUSSING AND SOLVING THE PROBLEM

Once the children understand the mechanics of a knock-out tournament, set the groups to work to find an answer.

You will probably find that some groups choose to make a diagram like the following:

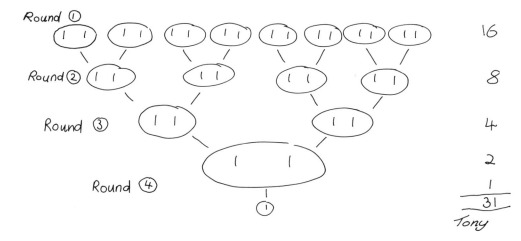

Others will work it out by halving, keeping a record of how many games are played in each round and then totalling these. Some might use counters to represent people and model the tournament, keeping a tally of the number of matches played. When the children have reached an answer, let groups share the way they worked out that 31 matches are played. Discuss which method was the quickest.

$$2\overline{)\overset{16}{32}}$$

$$+\quad 2\overline{)\overset{8}{16}}$$

$$+\quad 2\overline{)\overset{4}{8}}$$

$$2\overline{)\overset{2}{4}}$$

$$2\overline{)\overset{1}{2}}$$

$$\overline{31}$$

In the first ^round there is 16 matches
Second round there is 8 matches
Third round 4 matches
Forth round 2 matches
Finals 1 match

An Grade 5

BUILDING ON THE ACTIVITY

❏ Have children investigate how many matches would be played if there were 64 players in the draw (63 matches), using one of the methods from above. Ask the children if they can predict how many matches would be played if there were 16 players (15), and 128 players (127) and then have them work it out to check their predictions.

❏ Investigate what happens for a draw of 24 players. Is it possible? Why/why not? The children should work out that 3 players will be left in the draw, which is not a true knock-out situation.

❏ Can the children list the possible numbers of players for knock-out competitions? (2, 4, 8, 16, 32, 64, 128, 256 etc.)

It is good fun to organise a tournament for the class. To make sure that everyone gets a turn you may have to award some byes in the first round. The tournament could be held over 2 or 3 weeks. You can involve children in the scheduling of matches.

40 Round robins

If each child in our class plays checkers with everyone else, how many games will be played?

Curriculum links

This is a variation of the more familiar handshake problem, i.e. ten people shook hands with each other, how many handshakes were there? It is an example of a round-robin style of tournament where each competitor plays every other competitor once. By working out simpler problems first, the children can find a pattern which will help them solve situations such as this where larger numbers are involved.

DISCUSSING AND SOLVING THE PROBLEM

Ask the children to recall competitions or tournaments they have taken part in where each person plays every other person. This should be quite easy as most inter-school sports are organised this way. Tell the children that you are going to work out the problem by doing it with smaller numbers first.

Now tell the children to make groups of three and to act out the situation to find out how many games three people would play. Write this information on the chalkboard:

People	Games
3	3

Then put the children in groups of four and let them act out the same situation (or have one group of four act it out). Add this information to your chart:

People	Games
3	3
4	6

Repeat for groups of five, six, seven and eight and keep adding the information to the chart:

People	Games
3	3
4	6
5	10
6	15
7	21
8	28

Discuss the information you have collected so far and ask the children if they can see any patterns developing. Give the children time to look for patterns and discuss them with their group. If the groups are unable to see any patterns, let them continue working out the number of games for nine and ten people. Then give them some more time to look for patterns in the numbers. They may see that the number of games go up each time; that if you add the people and the games together you get the next number of games; that the adding pattern on the games side is + 3, + 4, + 5, + 6 etc.

Once the children can see a pattern, let each group use one or more of these patterns to find the answer to the problem. The answer will vary depending on the number of children in your class. Give each group time to tell how they worked out their answer.

BUILDING ON THE ACTIVITY

❑ Let groups of students plan a draw for six people for a round-robin tournament using the information you have collected so far. They will need to work out who plays who and the times for playing.

❑ Is it feasible to hold a round-robin checkers tournament for the whole class? Why/why not? How could we plan it so it doesn't take as long?

It may help to know the rule: Multiply the number of people by the number of people minus 1 (because everyone plays everyone except themselves), and then divide by 2 (because it takes two people to play each game). Easy!

2 What's missing?

Reproducible page

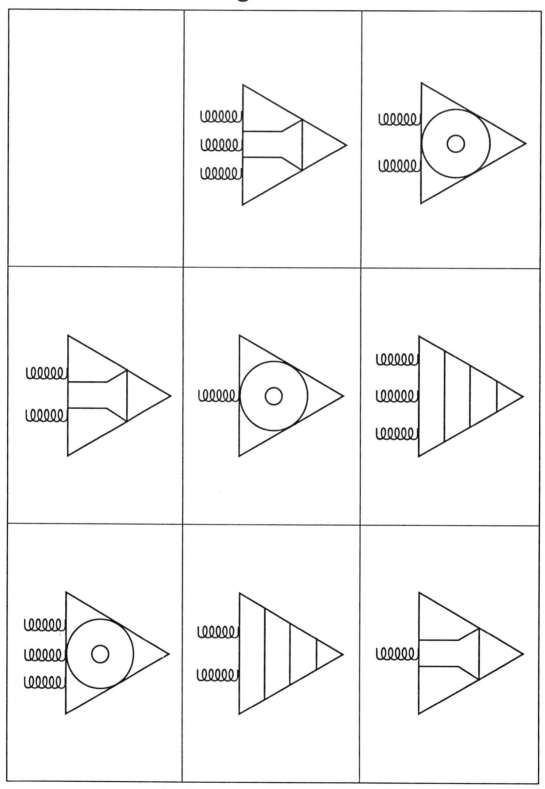

2 What's missing?

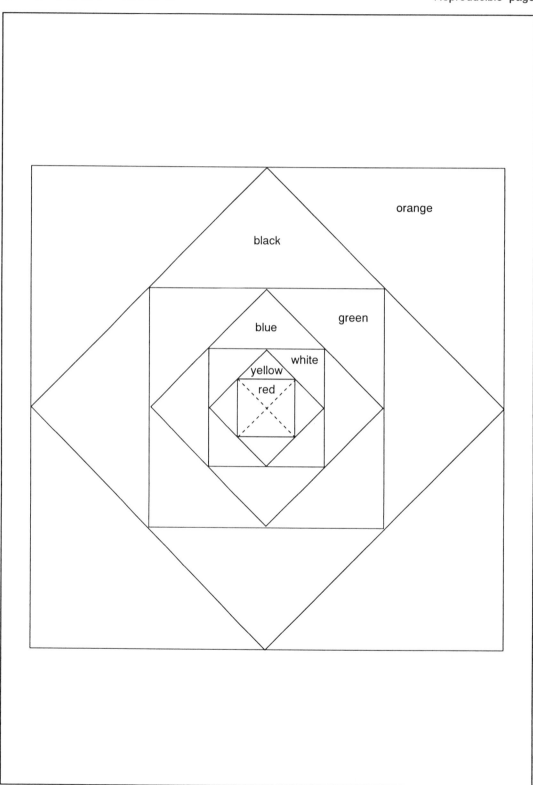

7 Ben's new clothes

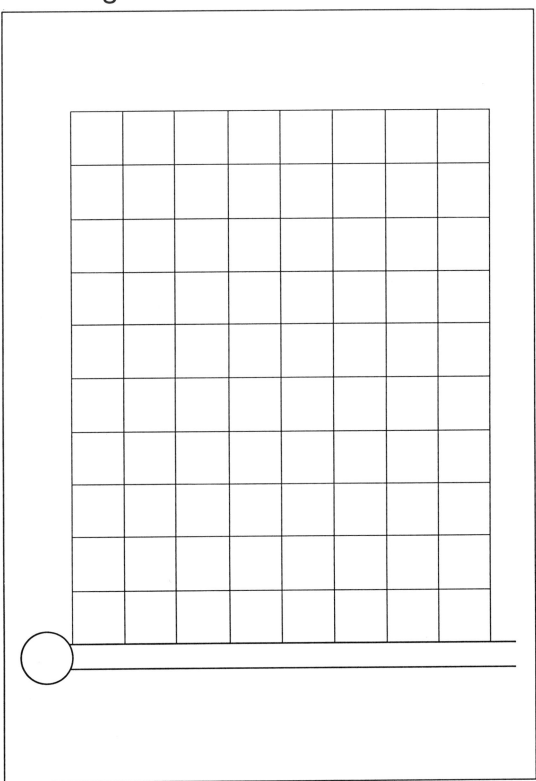

19 Duty rosters

←——— Morning ———→ ←——— Afternoon ———→

Grade 1

Grade 2

Grade 3

Grade 4

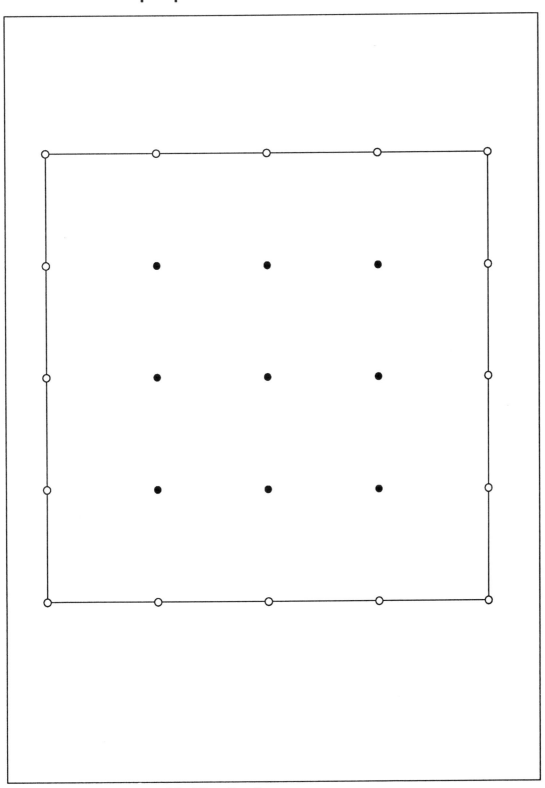

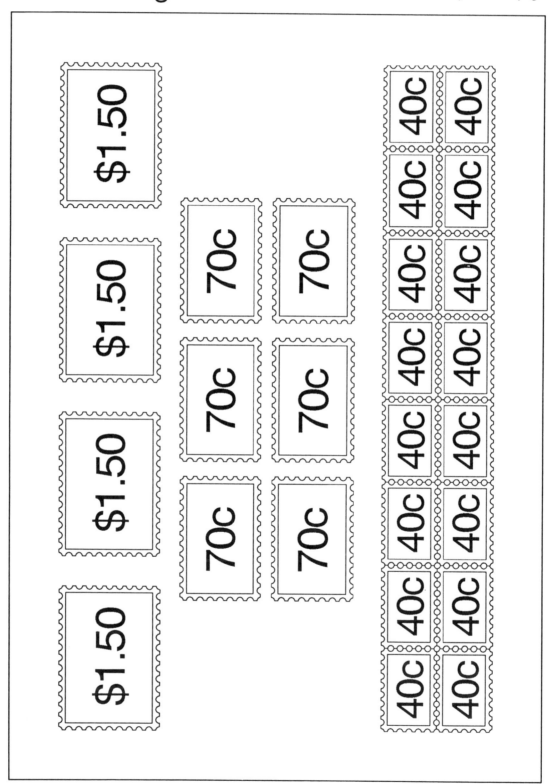

100 square

1	2	3	4	5	6	7	8	9	10
11	12	13	14	15	16	17	18	19	20
21	22	23	24	25	26	27	28	29	30
31	32	33	34	35	36	37	38	39	40
41	42	43	44	45	46	47	48	49	50
51	52	53	54	55	56	57	58	59	60
61	62	63	64	65	66	67	68	69	70
71	72	73	74	75	76	77	78	79	80
81	82	83	84	85	86	87	88	89	90
91	92	93	94	95	96	97	98	99	100

BIBLIOGRAPHY

A National Statement on Mathematics for Australian Schools. 1991. Australia: Curriculum Corporation.

Baker, Ann & Johnny. 1991. *Maths in the Mind.* Portsmouth, NH: Heinemann.

Dalton, Joan. 1992. *Adventures in Thinking.* Portsmouth, NH: Heinemann.

Meyer, Carol & Tom Sallee. 1983. *Make It Simpler.* Australia: Addison-Wesley.

Skinner, Penny. 1991. *What's Your Problem?* Portsmouth, NH: Heinemann.

Wilson, Jeni & Lynda Cutting. 1993. *It's Time: Celebrating Maths with Projects.* Portsmouth, NH: Heinemann.